THE FOUNDERS' SPEECH
TO SAVE AMERICA

THE FOUNDERS' SPEECH TO SAVE AMERICA

How The Founding Fathers
Defeated Tyranny

STEVEN RABB

PAPERBACK EDITION

ISBN

978-1-7358164-8-7

Copyright © 2024 Steven Rabb

All rights reserved. This book or any portion thereof may not be reproduced or used in any manner whatsoever without the express written permission of the publisher except for the use of brief quotations in a book review.

Printed by Liberty For All Publishers in the United States

Visit

www.TheFoundersUSA.com

Liberty For All Publishers
Atlanta, Georgia

For Phyllis Joann Meebold Rabb,

You gave yourself in the raising of we three children, and to the thousands of children you taught through the years as a gifted Christian Educator. Not through speeches, not in front of the crowds, but in the daily loving spirit, the example of service and grace, the hours of caring unnoticed, the encouragement when needed most, you were the best at the most important thing, and earned the greatest title any human can ever hold or aspire to; you were and are a wonderful mom. The poetry, the creativity, the ukulele, the pumpkin pie; for the laughter, for the Johnny Appleseed, for all of it, thank you mom. I love you.

*"If some faint love of goodness glow in me,
Pure spirit! I first caught that flame from thee."*

Steven Charles Rabb

(Mom lives with Alzheimer's and is in the loving care of my sister and brother-in-law, Cheryl and Mike Schulze, the strength of our family, and for whom my sister Lisa and I are eternally grateful.)

Acknowledgements

Without the love and support of my beautiful and loving wife, Shannon, this passion project would never have been completed. Without the encouragement of my amazing sons, Kevin and Connor, The Founders' Speech Series would never have started.

Special thanks to my editor, Jessica Mohr, who brings her deep faith, uncommon insights, and unparalleled professionalism to the editing of these books. Also special thanks to Kristina Konstantinova for her wonderful work on the formatting, Ghislain Viau for the cover design, and Josh Masterson for his contribution to the prologue.

Table of Contents

Acknowledgements VII

Table of Contents VIII

Author's Note XI

Prologue 1

Chapter One ..... Awakened 9

Chapter Two ..... Home 23

Chapter Three .. Foundations 34

Chapter Four ... Rights 46

Chapter Five ..... Tyrants 58

Chapter Six .... Insurrection 70

Chapter Seven .. United 82

Chapter Eight .. Declaration 99

Chapter Nine .... Republic 112

Chapter Ten ...... Posterity 131

A Parting Message From The Father of Our Nation 139

Index 149

Author's Note

The Founders' Speech To Save America is the story of the faith and works of the founding generation of Americans. I purposely use the term 'generation' to include the entire people and spirit of the era. A generation of people who united from across thirteen colonies to jealously guard their sacred rights. They stood up in unison not only to British tyrants, but to the elite loyalist Tories within their ranks. This book tells the story of how a people rose with one voice and defeated the greatest empire on earth to reclaim their God-given rights.

How does that happen? Where do people like that come from? That is where the book begins; with a glimpse into the faith, the families, and the foundations of a new civilization that would revolutionize the world.

Using their own words, the book is written as a speech. The quotes included are not only those of the Founding Fathers but also the words of those who inspired them, as well as many they inspired in the generations that followed. We all need to hear the power of their words and their amazing relevance to the issues we face today—perhaps now more than ever before.

As I crafted *The Founders' Speech To Save America*, I imagined the readers as part of an audience, standing in the back of a town hall meeting or sitting in a church pew, listening intently as the Founders' speech is delivered. I pictured *Scribe* at the front of the town hall or church, narrating the Founders' words with passion, as though speaking them for the first time.

To help the reader follow along, I have enumerated and italicized the author of each text in a superscript citation for immediate attribution. Several texts have been lightly curated for support of the narrative flow, pronoun consistency, and modern usage standards.

To fully understand the premise and enjoy the book, I encourage the reader to start with the Prologue.

Steven Rabb

Prologue

Providence has transported the Founding Fathers to the Assembly Room in Philadelphia's Independence Hall, in the midst of modern-day America. Their mission, as they understood it, was to write a speech to modern day America, *The Founders' Speech to a Nation in Crisis*, in order to recall the people to their founding principles and ethos.

But after the hours of debate and discussion in writing that first speech, they will soon learn their mission is not yet complete.

Seated around the Assembly Room the seven men remain immersed in conversation. Mr. Washington, tall and dignified, is in his customary place—a mahogany chair topped with the crest of the rising sun, positioned on a dais at the head of the room. The other six men sit at tables draped in heavy green wool and spaced evenly around the large chamber.

I, chosen as their Scribe, stand at the back of the room and note all that is said and done.

John Adams, as quick with words as he is to temper, speaks first. "We have completed our mission, Gentlemen." His sharp blue eyes, judging, scan the other men. "The work that remains is in the hands of the people, as it has always been."

"Agreed, Mr. Adams," says the stout and stooped Benjamin Franklin with practiced diplomacy. "The question that now remains is the character of the people."

"The debt of the nation as well, Mr. Franklin," Jefferson, tall and fit though no longer young, interjects. "That question also remains."

"Have you not found, Mr. Jefferson," asks Franklin in tones somehow both respectful and jocular—a balance few could muster but comes easily to America's first diplomat, "the character of the people and the debt of the nation to be inextricably connected?"

"So I have," Jefferson begrudgingly concedes. Then, with a glance at Hamilton, adds, "Issues of character, excessiveness, and debt were paramount in our time as well."

"And yet," Hamilton retorts, pale, dignified, and quick to riposte, "when some had a chance to extinguish the debt, they chose instead to double it."

Outside, rain begins to fall. Heavy drops tap on the windowsills. Trees sway as the wind picks up.

"Doubled the debt, yes. And the size of the country along with it!" Jefferson says directly, his voice defensive and rising. "The addition of nine self-governing states and the increase of our territory, Sir, was vital to the security of our people, and the defense of our —"

"Debtors," interrupts Hamilton, his tone sharp and dripping with disdain, "often cite security when excusing their vices. My point is that excuses do not trump the Constitution."

"*You* would lecture *me* on vices and spending?" asks Jefferson. "Is there no limit to your hubris? Or your innovations in the name of the general welfare? Your exuberance left our nation and its posterity in unfathomable debt. The usurpation of states rights in the name of one fancy after another!"

"The National Bank was such a fancy, Sir," says Hamilton, "to make possible your Louisiana Purchase."

"And for each good your Bank has done," asks Jefferson, "what numerous harms has it wrought? Your confidence in your own genius over the genius of the people is your downfall, Mr. Hamilton. It jeopardizes our nation!"

"And your states-first approach is yours, Mr. Jefferson! What did that colonies-only approach accomplish during our time? I mean, aside from leaving soldiers starved and shoeless as they fought for our liberty!"

"And yet they fought like men and won our liberty, Sir! Which patriots will always do within the limited role of the Federal—"

"Yes, Mr. Jefferson!" Hamilton says, standing so abruptly his chair clatters to the floor. "Yes, *we* patriots did fight. While some remained safely in their homes and—"

Jefferson quickly stands and steps toward Hamilton, "You insult my honor, Sir!"

"And you, mine!" Hamilton retorts as he steps closer.

"Gentlemen!" interrupts John Adams. Like the other men in the room, he seems embarrassed at his companions' fractiousness. "No duels today! We are here to save this country! Not lay each other low!"

Hamilton, brought short by Adams' words but too proud for apologies, gives Jefferson a long look.

Meeting Hamilton's glare, Jefferson takes several measured breaths, then returns to his desk.

While the emotions in the room are still settling, the short and slight James Madison asks,

"And where is Mr. Washington?"

All eyes move first to the Rising Sun Chair raised on its dais.

Seeing it empty, the men look around the room.

Madison, nearest the back, steps to the door, opens it, and looks into the passageway beyond.

Before he's even signaled that there's no sign of Washington, Hamilton is rushing to where the general had been sitting. He notes with clear relief that Washington hasn't fallen to the floor behind his table. He brushes the table's skirt as if checking beneath it. Flummoxed, he turns in a slow circle, clearly wondering where Mr. Washington could have disappeared to.

While consternation among the other men grows, Franklin moves to one of the large windows that face the front of the building.

When he speaks, the quiet sobriety of his voice brings all eyes to him. "I see him, gentlemen. He is there," Franklin says, motioning out the window and onto the grounds where wind-driven rain now falls in sheets.

The men rush to the windows, gathering to see if Mr. Washington is in danger.

"Is he harmed?" asks Hamilton. "I will go to him."

"Not necessary, Mr. Hamilton," Franklin says. He nods at a standing Washington, who looks slightly toward the heavens as the rain beats down on his face. "He appears to be praying."

"In the storm?"

"Is there a better time?" asks Franklin.

The question needs no response, and the men stand quietly, watching their general.

After some time, Franklin says to the window, as though not to disturb Washington, "I was a young man during the Great Awakening, when our states were still colonies. I was there when Mr. Whitefield preached tens of thousands from all sects and denominations into a deep, abiding faith. It was as though every man, woman, and child in this country were on their knees."

"The Great Awakening," agrees John Adams, "changed the sentiments of the people. I was just a boy when Mr. Whitefield came to Boston. And I have been a church going animal ever since."

Samuel Adams, in a reflective tone, quietly quotes 2 Chronicles 7:14: "If my people, who are called by my name, will humble themselves and pray and seek my face and turn from their wicked ways, then I will hear from heaven, and I will forgive their sin and will heal their land."

The rain beats down on the windows as we stand silent, reflecting on those words, when Franklin says, "Gentlemen, our work here is not finished. We have one more speech that must be written. Mr. Hamilton. Mr. Jefferson. Will you please go to the General?"

"Of course!" Hamilton says, already moving to the door. "I will guard him."

"No," says Jefferson, "we must bring him in from the storm—"

"Gentlemen," Franklin admonishes. "Go to him . . . wait on him . . . and perhaps join him."

And then to me, he adds, "Mr. Scribe, attend closely. We have more to say."

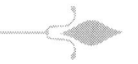

Directly I join Mr. Franklin.

"We all played our part in the forming of this country," Franklin continues, looking between Samuel and John Adams, "but you two gentlemen were there from the beginning in Boston where the tyranny was felt first and most. The faith of the people is the thing. The faith that brought our forefathers here and . . ."

At that moment a tremendous bolt of lightning strikes almost upon us, lighting the room and shaking it with a boom of thunder quickly upon it.

Mr. Franklin pauses and looks at me. "Mr. Scribe, please go to the General and ensure his safety and that of our friends."

I run at once outside to see they are unharmed. As I come to the double doors of the hall and look out onto the green, I see the General now on one knee, head bowed, with Mr. Hamilton and Mr. Jefferson standing on either side with heads bowed. I walk slowly up to them and hear Mr. Washington in prayer:

". . . Bless, O Lord, the whole race of mankind, and let the world be filled with the knowledge of Thee and Thy Son Jesus Christ. Pity the sick, the poor, the weak, the needy, and the widows, and all that mourn or are broken in heart. Be, O Lord, a Father to the fatherless, a Comforter to the comfortless, a Deliverer to the captives, and a Physician to the sick, and be merciful to them according to their several necessities.

"Bless all the people of this land, from the highest to the lowest, particularly those whom Thou has appointed to rule over us in church and state. I humbly beseech Thee to be merciful to me in the free pardon of my sins, for the sake of Thy dear Son, my only Savior, Jesus Christ, who came not to call the righteous, but sinners to repentance. Make me humble, meek, patient, and contented, and work in me the grace of Thy Holy Spirit so that into Thy hands I shall commend myself, both soul and body, in the name of Thy Son, Jesus Christ, beseeching Thee, when this life shall end. Amen."

As Washington's prayer ends, I return to the hall to make my report, but as I enter the hall I stop short, listening as Mr. Franklin instructs the other men.

"So we agree, we must speak of the faith of the founding generation, but Gentlemen, faith without works is dead, and you, Gentlemen," as he looks again to John and Samuel Adams, "led the patriots to resist tyranny in Boston. The people must understand how to defeat tyranny; they must unite to win back their liberty as the patriots of this nation did once before. Will you tell that story? Will you write that speech?"

"Of course Mr. Franklin," says John Adams. "But it was Samuel who lit the spark. I merely fanned the flames."

"Well my cousin," says Samuel, "is a man of many words, and fanned most of those flames with his breath."

The Founders laugh harder than the joke merits as they feel their tension replaced with relief and hope.

As if on cue, Washington, Hamilton, and Jefferson, sodden and chilled, reenter the room.

"Faith and works, Gentlemen. That is the speech," Franklin says, wiping tears from his wrinkled but still-keen eyes. "He turns to address the General. "Mr. Washington, your timing is impeccable as always. We are to write another speech: the faith of the people and the works of the patriots to defeat tyranny."

"I agree, Mr. Franklin," Washington says. "Our work here is not done. Truly, we must speak of the faith of the people. And we must speak of the works of the patriots who defeated tyranny. But Gentlemen, we must also speak of the unity that is required in a people who seek to preserve their liberty . . . and to that end, I have something I must say."

"Of course, Sir," Franklin says respectfully.

And with that the Founders return to their seats, and I to my pen, and through the night, I transcribe for these brothers in arms, "The Founders' Speech To Save America."

Chapter One
Awakened

[1] *WILLIAM BRADFORD* Being thus arrived in a good harbor and brought safely to land, they fell upon their knees and blessed the God of heaven who had brought them over the vast and furious ocean and delivered them from all the perils and miseries thereof, again to set their feet on the firm and stable earth—their proper element.

[2] *WILLIAM BRADFORD* Thus, out of small beginnings, greater things have been produced by His hand that made all things of nothing and gives being to all things that are; and, as one small candle may light a thousand, so the light here kindled hath shone unto many; yea, in some sort, to our whole nation. [3] *JOHN WINTHROP* For we must consider that we shall be as a city upon a hill. The eyes of all people are upon us. So that if we shall deal falsely with our God in this work we have undertaken, and so cause Him to withdraw His present help from us, we shall be made a story and a byword through the world.

[4] *JOSIAH QUINCY* My friends, the great, comprehensive truths, written on every page of our history, are these: human happiness has no perfect security but freedom; freedom, none but virtue; virtue, none but knowledge; and neither freedom nor virtue has any vigor or immortal hope, except in the principles of the Christian faith, and in the sanctions of the Christian religion.

[5] *CHARLES MAXSON* Sadly, the early eighteenth century was an age of passionless orthodoxy, of nominal and apologetic believers. [6] *JOSEPH TRACY* Boston had lost much of the power of religion. None had heard of any remarkable stir in it for many years. Ministers and people were obliged to confess that the love of many had waxed cold. Both seemed too much conformed to the world.

[7] *CHARLES MAXSON* In this cold, unsympathetic age, Mr. Whitefield awakened the mellowing and civilizing emotions, so that men had a strange, new passion for their fellows, as well as a new delight in their God. [8] *CHARLES MAXSON* The worldwide religious awakening was a countermovement. This new evangelism changed the lives of thousands and called into being the church within the church, a saving nucleus in almost every community, composed of divinely illuminated men.

[9] *BENJAMIN FRANKLIN* The multitudes of all sects and denominations that attended Mr. Whitefield's sermons were enormous. [10] *JONATHAN EDWARDS* The work was vastly beyond any former outpouring of the Spirit that ever was known. There has formerly sometimes been a remarkable awakening and success in the means of grace, in some particular congregations; and this used to be much taken notice of, and acknowledged to be glorious, though the towns and congregations round about continued dead: But now, God has brought to pass a new thing; He has wrought a revival of the people that has extended from one end of the land to the other.

SCRIBE In the late 1730s and early 1740s, when the Founding Fathers were young men or children, a revival of faith stirred the soul of the nation like never before. Three out of four colonists attended the hundreds of outdoor revivals as the Spirit of God swept through, bringing people together from every denomination, often in revival crowds of thousands and tens of thousands in number. This movement of God's Spirit became known as the Great Awakening.

[11] *BENJAMIN FRANKLIN* It was wonderful to see the change soon made in the manners of our inhabitants. From being thoughtless or indifferent about religion, it seemed as if all the world were growing religious, so that one could not walk through the town in an evening without hearing psalms sung in different families of every street. [12] *JONATHAN EDWARDS* The towns seemed to be full of the presence of God, and never were so full of love nor of joy. [13] *JONATHAN EDWARDS* There was great and continual commotion, day and night, and there was indeed a very great revival of religion.

[14] *BENJAMIN FRANKLIN* I was one of the number to observe the extraordinary influence of Mr. Whitefield's oratory on his hearers, and how much they admired and respected him, notwithstanding his common abuse of them, by assuring them that they were naturally half beasts and half devils. [15] *BENJAMIN FRANKLIN* Being among the hindmost in Market Street in Philadelphia, I had the curiosity to learn how far Mr. Whitefield could be heard, by retiring backwards down the street towards the Delaware River. And I found his voice distinct till I came near Front Street, when some noise in that street obscured it. Imagining, then, a semi-circle, of which my distance would be the radius, and that if it were filled with auditors, to each of whom I allowed two square feet, I computed that he might well be heard by more than thirty thousand. This reconciled me to the newspaper accounts of his having preached to twenty-five thousand people in the field.

[16] *PAUL SVININ* A big fair can convey a sufficient notion of the size of the crowd at such a meeting, but the sights that are to be seen here are more varied and stranger. These gatherings cannot be

likened either to a military camp or to the encampment of a nomadic horde. Often I imagined myself among the Israelites led by Moses into the land of Canaan. In the dark night, you see charming sights wherever you go. Century-old oaks and cedars are turned into dwelling places, lodgings are fashioned in the boughs, in which by the light of candles are seen rich viands† and feasting toilers, while under the trees, the preacher, amidst the night's darkness with his eloquence, works up his hearers into a fervor.

17 *NATHAN COLE* It was my hearing of his preaching at Philadelphia, like one of the old Apostles, with many thousands flocking to hear him preach the Gospel, and great numbers converted to Christ, that I felt the Spirit of God drawing me by conviction to see and hear Mr. Whitefield.

I soon heard he had come to New York and the Jerseys, and great multitudes were flocking after him under great concern for their souls, and many converted, which brought on my concern more and more, hoping soon to see him, but next I heard, he was at Long Island, then at Boston, and next at Northampton.

One day, all of a sudden, there came a messenger and said Mr. Whitefield preached at Hartford and Wethersfield yesterday and is to preach at Middletown this evening [October 23, 1740]. I was in my field at work. I dropped my tool that I had in my hand and ran home and ran through my house and bade my wife get ready quick to go and hear Mr. Whitefield preach at Middletown, and run to my pasture for my horse with all my might fearing that I would be too late to hear him.

I brought my horse home and soon mounted and took my wife

---

†   Viands: an item of food, provisions.

up and went forward as fast as I thought the horse could bear, and when my horse began to be out of breath, I would get down and put my wife on the saddle and bid her ride as fast as she could and not stop or slack for me except I bade her, and so I would run until I was much out of breath, and then mount my horse again. And so I did several times to favor my horse, we improved every moment to get along as if we were fleeing for our lives, all the while fearing we should be too late to hear the sermon, for we had twelve miles to ride double in little more than an hour.

And when we came within about half a mile of the road that comes down from Hartford, Wethersfield, and Stepney to Middletown, on high land, I saw before me a cloud or fog rising. I first thought it came from the great river, but as I came nearer to the road, I heard a noise— something like a low, rumbling thunder and presently found it was the noise of horses' feet coming down the road, and this cloud was a cloud of dust made by the horses' feet. It arose into the air over the tops of the hills and trees, and when I came within about twenty rods of the road, I could see men and horses slipping along in the cloud like shadows. As I drew nearer, it seemed like a steady stream of horses and their riders, scarcely a horse more than his length behind another, all of a lather and foam with sweat, their breath rolling out of their nostrils in the cloud of dust with every jump. Every horse seemed to go with all his might to carry his rider to hear news from heaven for the saving of souls. It made me tremble to see the sight, how the world was in a struggle. I found a vacancy between two horses to slip in my horse, and my wife said, "Our clothes will be all spoiled—see how they look?" For they were so covered with dust, that they looked almost all of one color: coats, hats, shirts, and horses.

We went down in the stream. I heard no man speak a word all the way three miles but every one pressing forward in great haste, and when we got to the old meeting house, there was a great multitude. It was said to be three or four thousands of people assembled together. We got off from our horses and shook off the dust, and the ministers were then coming to the meeting house. I turned and looked towards the great river and saw the ferry boats running swiftly forward and forward, bringing over loads of people. The oars rowed nimbly and quickly, everything, men, horses, and boats, seemed to be struggling for life. The land and banks over the river looked black with people and horses all along the twelve miles. I saw no man at work in his field, but all seemed to be gone.

When I saw Mr. Whitefield come upon the scaffold, he looked almost angelical: a young, slim, slender youth before some thousands of people with a bold, undaunted countenance. My hearing everywhere how God was with him as he came along solemnized my mind and put me into a trembling fear before he began to preach; for he looked as if he was clothed with authority from the great God, and a sweet solemnity sat upon his brow. And my hearing him preach gave me a heart wound; by God's blessing, my old foundation was broken up.

18 *GEORGE WHITEFIELD* Do you ask what I am doing? I answer: ranging and hunting in the American woods after poor sinners. 19 *GEORGE WHITEFIELD* Come away, my dear brethren. Fly, fly, fly for your lives to Jesus Christ! Fly to a bleeding God; fly to a throne of grace; and beg of God to break your heart; beg of God to convince you of your actual sins; beg of God to convince you of your original sin; beg of God to convince you of your self-righteousness; beg of God to give you faith, and to enable you to close with Jesus Christ!...

[20] JONATHAN EDWARDS It was very wonderful to see how persons' affections were sometimes moved—when God did, as it were, suddenly open their eyes and let into their minds a sense of the greatness of His grace, the fullness of Christ, and His readiness to save—after having been broken with apprehensions of divine wrath and sunken in an abyss under a sense of guilt, which they were ready to think was beyond the mercy of God.

[21] JONATHAN EDWARDS The minds of people were wonderfully taken off from the world. The world was treated amongst us as a thing of very little consequence. [22] JONATHAN EDWARDS After great convictions and humbling, and agonizing with God, they had Christ discovered to them anew as an all-sufficient Savior, and in the glories of His grace and in a far more clear manner than before; and with greater humility, self-emptiness, and brokenness of heart, and a purer, a higher joy, and greater desires after holiness of life; but with greater self-diffidence and distrust of their treacherous hearts.

[23] JONATHAN EDWARDS I suppose there is scarcely a minister in this land but from Sabbath to Sabbath used to pray that God would pour out His spirit, and work a reformation and revival of religion in this nation. And now when so great and extensive a reformation is so suddenly and wonderfully accomplished, in those very things that we have sought God for, shall we not acknowledge it? Or when we do, do it with great coldness, caution, and reserve?

[24] JOHN ADAMS What do we mean by the American Revolution? Do we mean the American war? The revolution was effected before the war commenced. The revolution was in the minds and hearts of the people—a change in their religious sentiments, of their duties and obligations. This radical change in the principles, opinions, sentiments, and affections of the people—this was the real American Revolution. [25] JOHN ADAMS For the general principles

on which the Fathers achieved independence, were the only principles in which that beautiful assembly of young gentlemen could unite. And what were these general principles? I answer: the general principles of Christianity.

26 JOHN CHAMBERS No candid observer will deny that whatever of good there may be in our American civilization is the product of Christianity. Still less can he deny that the grand motives which are working for the elevation and purification of our society are strictly Christian. The immense energies of the Christian church, stimulated by a love that shrinks from no obstacle, are all bent toward this great aim of universal purification. These millions of sermons and exhortations, which are a constant power for good, these countless prayers and songs of praise, on which the heavy-laden lift their hearts above the temptations and sorrows of the world, are all the product of faith in Jesus Christ. That which gives us protection by day and by night—the dwellings we live in, the clothes we wear, the institutions of social order—all these are the direct offspring of Christianity. All that distinguishes us from the pagan world, all that makes us what we are, and all that stimulates us in the task of making ourselves better than we are, is Christian. A belief in Jesus Christ is the very fountainhead of everything that is desirable and praiseworthy in our civilization, and this civilization is the flower of time. Humanity has reached its noblest thrift, its grandest altitudes of excellence, its high-water mark through the influence of this faith.

27 JOSEPH STORY In America, you may meet with towns unfortified, illiterate, and without the conveniences of habitations; but a people wholly without religion no traveler hath yet seen; and a city might as well be erected in the air as a state be made to unite where no divine worship is attended. Religion is the cement

of civil union and the essential support of legislation. No free government now exists in the world unless where Christianity is acknowledged and is the religion of the country. So far from Christianity, as some say, being part of the machinery necessary to despotism, the reverse is the fact. Christianity is part of the common law of this state. It is not proclaimed by the commanding voice of any human superior, but expressed in the calm and mild accents of customary law. Its foundations are broad and strong and deep; they are laid in the authority, the interest, and the affections of the people. Waiving all questions of the hereafter, it is the purest system of morality, the firmest auxiliary, and only stable support of all human laws. It is impossible to administer the laws without taking the religion which the defendant in error has scoffed at—that Scripture which he has reviled—as their basis; to lay aside these is at least to weaken the confidence in human veracity so essential to the purposes of society, and without which no question of property could be decided and no criminal brought to justice. A man taking an oath in the common form, on a discredited book, would be a most idle ceremony.

28 *GOUVERNEUR MORRIS* The most important of all lessons is the denunciation of ruin to every state that rejects the precepts of religion. There must be religion. 29 *DANIEL WEBSTER* For if the Bible is not widely circulated among the masses in this country, I do not know what is going to become of us as a nation. If truth be not diffused, then error will be. If God and His Word are not known and received, the devil and his works will gain the ascendency. If the evangelical volume does not reach every hamlet, the pages of a corrupt and licentious literature will. If the power of the Gospel is not felt throughout the length and breadth of this land, anarchy and misrule, degradation and misery, corruption and darkness, will reign without mitigation or end.

30 *ABRAHAM LINCOLN* Friends, the Bible is the best gift God has given to man. 31 *BENJAMIN RUSH* It is the only correct map of the human heart that ever has been published. 32 *BENJAMIN RUSH* In proportion as mankind adopts its principles, and obeys its precepts, they will be wise and happy.

33 *JOSEPH STORY* The promulgation of the great doctrines of religion, the being, and attributes, and providence of one Almighty God; the responsibility to Him for all our actions, founded upon moral freedom and accountability; a future state of rewards and punishments; the cultivation of all the personal, social, and benevolent virtues—these never can be a matter of indifference in any well-ordered community.

34 *CALVIN COOLIDGE* My friends, Christianity is the foundation of our society. Our governments rest so much on the teachings of the Bible that it would be difficult to support them if faith in these teachings would cease to be practically universal in our country. 35 *JOSEPH STORY* It is, indeed, difficult to conceive how any civilized society can well exist without them.

36 *GEORGE WASHINGTON* I believe it is impossible to account for the creation of the universe without the agency of a supreme Being.

37 *GEORGE WASHINGTON* I believe that God is that great and glorious Being, who is the beneficent Author of all the good that was, that is, or that will be.

38 *ROGER SHERMAN* I believe that there is one only living and true God, existing in three persons: the Father, the Son, and the Holy Ghost.

39 *ROGER SHERMAN* I believe that God did send His own Son to become

man, die in the room† and stead of sinners, and thus to lay a foundation for the offer of pardon and salvation to all mankind, so as all may be saved who are willing to accept the Gospel offer.

40 *JOHN HANCOCK* I believe we must confess our sins, resolve to forsake them, and implore the forgiveness of God through the merits of the Savior of the world.

41 *THOMAS JEFFERSON* I believe the precepts of Jesus as delivered by Himself, to be the most pure, benevolent, and sublime which have ever been preached to man.

42 *BENJAMIN RUSH* I believe the Gospel of Jesus Christ prescribes the wisest rules for just conduct in every situation of life.

43 *JAMES MADISON* I believe that belief in God, all-powerful, wise, and good, is essential to the moral order of the world and to the happiness of man.

44 *JOHN ADAMS* I believe that without religion, this world would be something not fit to be mentioned in polite company; I mean Hell.

45 *DANIEL WEBSTER* If we and our posterity shall be true to the Christian religion; if we and they shall live always in the fear of God and shall respect His commandments; if we and they shall maintain just, moral sentiments and such conscientious convictions of duty as shall control the heart and life, then we may have the highest hopes of the future fortunes of the country. And if we maintain those institutions of government and that political union, exceeding as it does all former examples of political associations, we may be sure of one thing: that while our country furnishes material for a thousand masters of the historical art, it will

† Room: in the space of.

have no decline and fall. It will go on prospering and to prosper.

But if we and our posterity reject religious institutions and authority, violate the rules of eternal justice, trifle with the injunctions of morality, and recklessly destroy the political constitution which holds us together, no man can tell how sudden a catastrophe may overwhelm us that shall bury all our glory in profound obscurity.

46 *JONATHAN EDWARDS* There is naturally a great enmity in the heart against vital religion, and there was a great deal of opposition against the glorious work of God in the Awakening. 47 *JONATHAN EDWARDS* And as this work goes on and spreads much in the world, so as to begin to shake kingdoms and nations, it will dreadfully stir up the rage of earth and Hell and will put the world into the greatest uproar.

48 *GEORGE WHITEFIELD* Though all things are calm now, the storm is gathering and by and by, it will break; it is at present no bigger than a man's hand. But when it is full, it will break, and then you will see whether you are found Christians or not. For it is easy to follow Christ when all things are safe. Yet your love to Jesus Christ would be seen more if you must lose your lives or deny your Jesus. It would be a trial of your love, when fire and faggot† were before you, if you would rush into that rather than fly from the truth as it is in Jesus.

49 *TIMOTHY DWIGHT* You already know what is to be done and the manner in which it is to be done. You need not be told that you are to use all efforts of your own, and to look humbly and continually to God to render those efforts successful; that you are to

---

†   Faggot: a bundle of sticks.

resist carefully and faithfully every approaching temptation and every rising sin; that you are to resolve on newness of life, and to seize every occasion, as it presents itself, to honor God and to bless your fellow men; that you are strenuously to contend against evil habits and watchfully to cherish good ones; and that you are constantly to aim at uniformity and eminency in a holy life, and to "adorn the doctrine of God our Savior in all things."

Individuals are often apt to consider their own private conduct as of small importance to the public welfare. This opinion is wholly erroneous and highly mischievous. On the contrary, the advantages to the public of private virtue, faithful prayer, and edifying example, cannot be calculated. No one can conjecture how many will be made better, safer, and happier, by the virtue of one. This is the way in which the chief good, ever placed in the power of most persons, is to be done. Few persons can be concerned in settling systems of faith, molding forms of government, regulating nations, or establishing empires. But almost all can train up a family for God; instill piety, justice, kindness and truth; distribute peace and comfort around a neighborhood; receive the poor and the outcast into their houses; tend the bed of sickness; pour balm into the wounds of pain; and awaken a smile in the aspect of sorrow. In the secret and lowly vale of life, virtue in its most lovely attire delights to dwell. There God, with peculiar complacency, most frequently finds the inestimable ornament of a meek and quiet spirit.

Among the particular duties required by this precept, none holds a higher place than the observation of the Sabbath. The Sabbath and its ordinances have ever been the great means of all moral good to mankind. The faithful observation of the sabbath is, therefore, one of the chief duties and interests of men.

I have been credibly informed that an eminent philosopher declared that Christianity would be exterminated from the American colonies within a century from this time. The opinion has doubtless been often declared and extensively imbibed; and has probably furnished our enemies their chief hopes of success. For where religion prevails, their system cannot succeed. Where religion prevails, Illuminatism cannot make disciples, a French Jacobin cannot govern, a nation cannot be made slaves, nor villains, nor atheists, nor beasts. To destroy us, therefore, in this dreadful sense, our enemies must first destroy our Sabbath and seduce us from the house of God.

The Sabbath with its ordinances constitutes the bond of union to Christians, the badge by which they know each other; their rallying point; the standard of their host. In no way can we so preserve, or so announce to others, our character as Christians. Now more than ever, we are "not to be ashamed of the gospel of Christ." Now more than ever, are we to stand forth to the eye of our enemies, and of the world, as open, determined Christians. Now more than ever, are we to awaken our faith and declare ourselves as followers of Christ. *SCRIBE* Now more than ever.

Chapter Two
Home

[1] *THOMAS PAINE* Though I appear a sort of wanderer, the married state has not a sincerer friend than I am. It is the harbor of human life and is, with respect to the things of this world, what the next world is to this. It is home; and that one word conveys more than any other word can express. [2] *ABRAHAM LINCOLN* Here in my heart, my happiness, my house. Here inside the lighted window is my love, my hope, my life. Peace is my companion on the pathway winding to the threshold. Inside this portal dwells new strength in the security, serenity, and radiance of those I love above life itself. Here, two will build new dreams, dreams that tomorrow will come true. The world over, these are the thoughts at eventide when footsteps turn ever homeward. In the haven of the hearthside is rest and peace and comfort.

[3] *LYDIA SIGOURNEY* The strength of a nation, especially of a republican nation, is in the intelligent and well-ordered homes of the people. [4] *J.G. HOLLAND* For in the homes of America are born the children of America; and from them go out into American life, American men and women. They go out with the stamp of these homes upon them, and only as these homes are what they should be will they be what they should be.

[5] *JOHN ADAMS* The very fabric of American society hinges upon the

integrity and fidelity nurtured within family units. 6 *EDMUND BURKE* To be attached to the subdivision, to love the little platoon we belong to in society, is the first principle—the germ, as it were—of public affections. It is the first link in the series by which we proceed towards a love to our country and to mankind. The interest of that portion of social arrangement is a trust in the hands of all those who compose it. None but bad men would justify it in abuse; none but traitors would barter it away for their own personal advantage.

7 *STEPHEN FIELD* No legislation can be supposed more wholesome and necessary in the founding of a free, self-governing commonwealth than that which seeks to establish it on the basis of the idea of the family, as consisting in and springing from the union for life of one man and one woman in the holy estate of matrimony—the sure foundation of all that is stable and noble in our civilization and the best guarantee of reverent morality.

8 *ROBERT MORRIS* There is no relation on this side of the grave more sacred, more dignified, or more elevated, than that of husband and wife. 9 *THOMAS AQUINAS* It is the force that welds society together. 10 *AUGUSTINE OF HIPPO* By its means, sins are forgiven. By its means, the peace of a family is restored. By its means, man and wife are heirs together of the grace of life. 11 *THOMAS AQUINAS* For marriage is the sacrament of love, the sign of unity, the bond of charity, a symbol of Christ and the Church.

12 *JOHN ADAMS* The bedrock of national morality rests within private families. No matter how diligently schools, academies, and universities are established, their efforts are in vain if children are imbued with loose principles and licentious habits from their earliest years. How can children grasp the sacred obligations of morality and religion when they witness their mothers habitually

unfaithful to their fathers, and vice versa? [13] *SAMUEL WILLIAMS* Or when wealth is the great object? Or when marriage becomes a matter of trade, pride, and form? Or when affection, virtue, and happiness are not consulted? [14] *ROBERT MORRIS* Or when the demon-spirit of an evil temper is constantly manifested? Or when a shrill, harsh voice of complaint is perpetually ringing in the ear of one or the other? Or when a disposition to find fault without cause, and thus to annoy and irritate, is constantly apparent? Or when the husband regards himself as a despot and treats his wife as a slave? Or when the wife, on the other hand, is constantly exacting and never striving to discharge her part in the harmonious obligations? The effects are bitter, painful, and in every way melancholy. [15] *SAMUEL WILLIAMS* In such instances, the parties derive no felicity, and society receives no advantage. For it is only where the moral laws of nature lead the way that all the lovely train of virtues, domestic happiness, and the greatest of all public benefits are found to be the fruit.

[16] *GEORGE ELIOT* What greater thing is there for two human souls than to feel that they are joined for life to strengthen each other in all labor, to rest on each other in all sorrow, to minister to each other in all pain; [17] *ROBERT MORRIS* that they might be, and should be, to each other, perpetual sources of consolation and pleasure; no distrust, no suspicion, no equivocation should exist between beings so circumstanced. They should live as much as possible as if animated by one soul and aiming at one destiny; [18] *GEORGE ELIOT* to be one with each other in silent, unspeakable memories at the moment of the last parting.

[19] *JOHN ADAMS* Oh my dear Abigail, I thank Heaven that another fortnight will restore you to me—after so long a separation. My soul and body have both been thrown into disorder by your absence,

and a month or two more would make me the most insufferable cynic in the world. I see nothing but faults, follies, frailties and defects in anybody lately. People have lost all their good properties, or I, my justice or discernment. But you who have always softened and warmed my heart shall restore my benevolence as well as my health and tranquility of mind. You shall polish and refine my sentiments of life and manners, banish all the unsocial and ill-natured particles in my composition, and form me to that happy temper.

20 *ALEXANDER HAMILTON* Truth is, I cannot be absent from you, my dear Eliza, and my darling little ones. I feel that nothing can ever compensate for the loss of the enjoyments I leave at home or can ever put my heart at tolerable ease. In reality, my attachments to home disqualify me for either business or pleasure abroad and the prospect of a detention here for eight or ten days, perhaps a fortnight, fills me with an anxiety which will best be conceived by my Betsey's own impatience. Think of me with as much tenderness as I do of you, and we cannot fail to be always happy.

21 *GEORGE WASHINGTON* You may believe me, my dear Patsy, when I assure you in the most solemn manner, that so far from seeking this appointment, I have used every endeavor in my power to avoid it, not only from my unwillingness to part with you and the family, but from a consciousness of its being a trust too great for my capacity, and that I should enjoy more real happiness and felicity in one month with you at home than I have the most distant prospect of reaping abroad, if my stay were to be seven times seven years.

22 *JOHN ADAMS* When I went home to my family in May, 1770, from the town meeting in Boston, which was the first I had ever attended, and where I had been chosen in my absence, without any solicitation, one of their representatives, I said to my wife, "I have

accepted a seat in the House of Representatives, and thereby have consented to my own ruin, to your ruin, and to the ruin of our children. I give you this warning, that you may prepare your mind for your fate." She burst into tears, but instantly cried out in a transport of magnanimity, "Well, I am willing in this cause to run all risks with you and be ruined with you, if you are ruined!"

[23] *CHARLES INGERSOLL* The dealings between men and women in some countries is confined by cold and haughty customs, almost to the circles of consanguinity.† In others, from opposite causes, it is unrestrained, voluptuous, and depraved. In the United States, it is free, chaste, and honorable. Women are said to afford a type of the state of civilization. In savage life, they are slaves. At the middle era of refinement, they are companions. With its excess, they become mistresses and slaves again. North America is now at that happy mean, when well-educated and virtuous women enjoy the confidence of their husbands, the reverence of their children, and the respect of society, which is chiefly indebted to them for its tone and embellishments.

[24] *ALEXIS DE TOCQUEVILLE* I have shown how democracy destroys or modifies the different inequalities that originate in society; but is this all, or does it not ultimately affect that great inequality of man and woman which has seemed, up to the present day, to be eternally based in human nature? I believe that the social changes that bring nearer to the same level the father and son, the aristocrat and the servant, and, in general, superiors and inferiors, will raise woman and make her more and more the equal of man. But here, more than ever, I feel the necessity of making myself clearly understood, for there is no subject on which the coarse

---

† The quality or state of being blood relations.

and lawless fancies of our age have taken a freer range.

There are people in Europe who, confounding together the different characteristics of the sexes, would make man and woman into beings not only equal, but alike. They would give to both the same functions and impose on both the same duties. They would mix them in all things—their occupations, their pleasures, their business. It may readily be conceived that by thus attempting to make one sex equal in all things to the other, both are degraded, and from so preposterous a medley of the works of nature nothing could ever result but weak men and disorderly women.

It has often been remarked that in Europe a certain degree of contempt lurks even in the flattery which men lavish upon women. Although a European frequently affects to be the slave of woman, it may be seen that he never sincerely thinks her his equal. In the United States, men seldom compliment women in such a manner, but they daily show how much they esteem them. They constantly display an entire confidence in the understanding of a wife and a profound respect for her freedom. They have decided that her mind is just as fitted as that of a man to discover the plain truth and her heart as firm to embrace it, and they have never sought to place her virtue, any more than his, under the shelter of prejudice, ignorance, and fear.

The Americans do not think that man and woman have either the same duties, yet consider both of them as beings of equal value. They do not give to the courage of woman the same form or the same direction as to that of man, but they never doubt her courage; and if they hold that man and his partner may not always exercise their intellect and understanding in the same manner, they at least believe the understanding of the one to be as sound as that of the other and her intellect to be as clear. Thus, then, Americans appear to me to have excellently understood the true principle of democratic improvement, and I have nowhere seen woman occupying a loftier position. If I were asked to what singular prosperity and growing strength of the American people ought mainly to be attributed, I should reply: to the superiority of their women.

25 *ABRAHAM LINCOLN* The greatest lessons I have ever learned were at my mother's knees: 26 *JOSEPH STORY* To soften firmness into mercy and chasten honor into refinement; to exalt generosity as a virtue; by a soothing care, to allay the anguish of the body and the far worse anguish of the mind; by her tenderness, to disarm passion; by her purity, to triumph over sense; to cheer the scholar sinking under his toil; to console the statesman for the ingratitude of a mistaken people; to visit the forsaken and to attend the neglected when counselors betray, justice persecutes, and brethren and disciples flee; and to exhibit in this lower world a type of that love, pure, constant and ineffable, which in another world we are taught to believe the test of virtue—such is her vocation.

27 *SAMUEL GOODRICH* Mothers, when you have a child on your knee, listen a moment. Do you know what that child is? It is an immortal being, destined to live forever. You who gave it birth, the mother of its body, are also the mother of its soul for good or for ill. Its character is yet undecided; its destiny is placed in your hands; 28 *JOSEPH STORY* to inspire those principles, to inculcate those doctrines, to animate those sentiments which generations yet unborn, and nations yet uncivilized, shall learn to bless. It is the couch of the tortured sufferer, the prison of the deserted friend, the cross of the rejected Savior—these are the theaters on which your greatest triumphs will be achieved.

29 *LYDIA SIGOURNEY* From the age of three, I was put to sleep in a

chamber by myself. There was no person in the family to whom it was convenient or fitting to be either my guard or companion. I was always attended to my pillow by maternal love, and then left alone, sometimes 'ere the last rays of the summer sun had entirely forsaken the landscape. But I felt no fear; false stories had never been told to frighten me. There was nothing to be afraid of "Our Father in Heaven," to whom the last words of closing day were said. He seemed near, and I fell asleep, as on His protecting arm. It might have been in some measure owing to this nightly solitude, that thought so early became my friend. In the intervals not given to sleep it talked with me. So delightful were its visits, that waited for and wooed it, and was displeased if slumber invaded or superseded the communion. For it sometimes brought me harmonies and thrilled me to strange delight with rhythmical words.

So much had I been inured to the measured dignity, and even solemnity, of books and literature in my early years that I would climb by the aid of a high, straight-backed chair, to the upper alcove of an old-fashioned dark mahogany bookcase, to discover if happily some stray volume had eluded previous explorations. The largest volume in my father's possession was a heavy folio of more than eight hundred pages, containing the works of the Rev. Matthew Henry, discourses, essays, tracts, and biographies. I believe it was the size of the book alone that inspired my ambition to master its contents. Yet impatiently bending over those pages, instinct with piety and baptized by prayer, methought a secret influence sometimes stole over me, moving me to lowliness and the love of God.

The sanctity of the Sabbath, as I saw it observed by those whom I most loved and respected, had an efficient and salutary power upon the forming character. There was under our roof no young or light-minded person to tempt me to "think my own thoughts, or speak my own words" on that consecrated day. "Remember, and keep it holy," was the sound in my heart at its earliest dawn. How quiet was everything around in that rural home, and what serene sobriety sat on every face.

I often rode to our temple of worship, overshadowed by steep, dark cliffs, which to my solemnized eyes were as Sinai, whence the law was given. Within these hallowed walls everything seemed most sacred. Words could not express the reverence with which I listened to the deep, and rather monotonously intoned voice of the pastor. Of those who occasionally exchanged with him, I took great note by way of comparison and contrast. Some of them, methought, exhibited the mild graces of the sage who drank the hemlock, and in others I traced the lineaments of the lamenting and reproving prophet, when he exclaimed, "The crown is fallen from our head—woe unto us! For we have sinned!"

Truly happy was my childhood, fed on dews of love, yet guarded from the evils of indulgence by habits of industry, order, and obedience which my parents wisely inculcated. My mother solemnly and permanently influenced my unfolding mind and heart. Dignified in person, with the commanding yet courteous manner, her powerful intellect was strengthened by familiarity with the best authors. Fullness of benevolence and a pervading piety melted any pride and made her the loving disciple of the Savior, in whom she early believed.

To my eye she was the model of perfect beauty, for I beheld her through a heart that was all her own. In her parlor, seated in her cushioned chair, by the side of a brightly blazing wood fire, she might often be seen, her knitting bag hanging near and a book open before her. Her sole companion might be a slender child, with an unusually fair complexion:

"Lydia, come here," whereupon the tiny personage descends from her perch near the bookshelf with uncommon velocity and ensconces herself in a tiny green armchair at her feet, ready for any wish that should be expressed.

"Read me these two pages of Young's 'Night Thoughts,' my dear, and be sure to pronounce every word slowly and distinctly."

Let no child think this was a hardship. To please one so beloved, or to win her smile, her approbation was sufficient happiness. Sometimes this call would be not to read aloud, but to sing. Her voice, which was in conversation an echo of the Soul's Harmony, a power in music, which she had been taught scientifically when a child. Many were the pieces in which I was instructed to accompany her, sacred, patriotic, or pathetic.

"My child, shall it be 'Pompey's Ghost to his Wife Cornelia,' or 'While Shepherds Watched Their Flocks by Night,' or 'The Poor, Distracted Lady,' or 'Indulgent Parents, Dear,' or 'Solitude'?"

The last-named one was often my selection; the sweet tune and the flowing words of the lyric are still fresh in memory. Did space allow, I would gladly copy the whole, which I have never seen in print. And as I inscribe these few words, there comes with them such gush of happiness, such a thrill of melody, as though an angel hovered near. May it not be so? For to her, who there worships among an innumerable company redeemed from the earth, I would humbly say in better words than my own:

> If some faint love of goodness glow in me,
> Pure spirit! I first caught that flame from thee.

[30] GEORGE WASHINGTON All I am, I owe to my mother. I attribute my success in life to the moral, intellectual, and physical education I

received from her.

SCRIBE On Tuesday, April 14, 1789, George Washington received official notification that he had been elected the first President of the United States. Before leaving for New York, the seat of government at that time, he insisted on visiting his ailing mother, Mary Washington. His adult grandson, George Washington Parke Custis, recorded what would be the last visit between the father of our nation and his mother:

31 *GEORGE WASHINGTON PARKE CUSTIS* An affected scene ensued. The son feelingly remarked the ravages which a torturing disease [cancer] had made upon the aged frame of his mother, and addressed her with these words:

32 *GEORGE WASHINGTON* The people, madam, have been pleased, with the most flattering unanimity, to elect me to the chief magistracy of these United States. But before I can assume the functions of my office, I have come to bid you an affectionate farewell. So soon as the weight of public business, which must necessarily attend the outset of a new government, can be disposed of, I shall hasten to Virginia, and— (here, the matron interrupted with . . .)

33 *MARY WASHINGTON*—and you will see me no more, my son; my great age, and the disease which is fast approaching my vitals, warn me that I shall not be long in this world. I trust in God that I may be somewhat prepared for the better world . . . But go, George, fulfill the high destinies which Heaven appears to have intended for you; go, my son, and may that Heaven's and Mother's blessing be with you always.

Chapter Three
Foundations

1 DANIEL WEBSTER If we work upon marble, it will perish; if we work upon brass, time will efface it; if we rear temples, they will crumble into dust; but if we work upon immortal minds and instill into them just principles, we are then engraving that upon tablets which no time will efface but will brighten and brighten to all eternity.

2 GEORGE WASHINGTON The best means of forming a manly, virtuous, and happy people will be found in the right education of youth. Without this foundation, every other means, in my opinion, must fail. *3 HENRY WARD BEECHER* For no matter how good the walls and the materials are, if the foundations are not strong, the building will not stand. By and by, in some upper room, a crack will appear. And men will say, "There is the crack, but the cause is the foundation." So if, in youth, you lay the foundation of your character wrongly, the penalty will be sure to follow.

4 NOAH WEBSTER My friends, the virtues of men are of more consequence to society than their abilities; for this reason, the heart should be cultivated with more assiduity than the head. *5 JOHN LOCKE* For virtue is harder to be got than a knowledge of the world; and, if lost in the young, is seldom recovered.

6 EMERSON WHITE The most dangerous transition in a youth's life is that which carries him from the authoritative control of the family and the school to the responsibility of untried liberty. The shores of this perilous strait of human life are strewn with wrecked manhood. The home-life and the school-life of the child should prepare the youth for this transition to freedom by effective training in self-control and self-guidance, and, to this end, the will must be disciplined by an increasing use of motives that quicken the sense of right and make the conscience regal.

7 *NATHANAEL GREENE* Here then lies the foundation of civil liberty: in forming the habits of the youthful mind, to fix in them the right ideas of benevolence, humanity, integrity, and truth; 8 *GOUVERNEUR MORRIS* to form them to good manners; to accustom them to labor; to inspire them with a love of order; and to impress them with respect for lawful authority. 9 *DANIEL WEBSTER* We must lay hold on the myriads of juvenile spirits before they have time to grow up, through ignorance, into a reckless hostility to social order; train them to sense and good morals; and inculcate the principles of religion, simply and solemnly.

10 *BENJAMIN RUSH* I will go further still. The only foundation for a useful education in a republic is to be laid in religion. Without this there can be no virtue, and without virtue there can be no liberty; and liberty is the object and life of all republican governments. We waste so much time and money in punishing crimes and take so little pains to prevent them. We profess to be republicans, and yet we neglect the only means of establishing and perpetuating our republican forms of government—that is, the universal education of our youth in the principles of Christianity by means of the Bible. For this divine book above all others favors that equality among mankind, that respect for just laws, and those sober and frugal virtues which constitute the soul of republicanism.

11 *DANIEL WEBSTER* Our ancestors established their system of

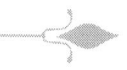

government on morality and religious sentiment. Moral habits, they believed, cannot safely be trusted on any other foundation than religious principle, nor any government secure that which is not supported by moral habits; that whatever makes men good Christians, makes them good citizens.

12 PATRICK HENRY My friends, bad men cannot make good citizens. It is impossible that a nation of infidels or idolaters should be a nation of freemen. For it is when a people forget God that tyrants forge their chains.

13 SAMUEL ADAMS What then is to be done? Let divines and philosophers, statesmen and patriots unite their endeavors to renovate the age by impressing the minds of men with the importance of educating their little boys and girls; of inculcating in the minds of youth the fear and love of the deity and universal philanthropy, and in subordination to these great principles, the love of their country; of instructing them in the art of self-government, without which they never can act a wise part in the government of societies great, or small; in short, of leading them in the study and practice of the exalted virtues of the Christian system, which will happily tend to subdue the turbulent passions of men.

14 DAVID SWING Some hold that too much stress has been laid on the moral sense, and that what men now most need is cultured intellect. A favorite maxim with this class of thinkers is that the human intellect contains within itself the germs of goodness which will generally increase with its intellectual growth. 15 DANIEL WEBSTER They are quite certain that the Christian religion is not the only true foundation, or any necessary foundation, of morals. The ground taken is that religion is not necessary to morality; that benevolence may be ensured by habit; and that all the virtues may flourish and be safely left to the chance of

flourishing without touching the waters of the living spring of religious responsibility.

16 *GOUVERNEUR MORRIS* These reformers have taken genius instead of reason for their guide, have adopted experiment instead of experience, and have wandered in the dark because they prefer lightning to light. 17 *EDMUND BURKE* Unmindful of what they have received from their ancestors or of what is due to their posterity, they act as if they were the entire masters; destroying at their pleasure the whole original fabric of their society; hazarding to leave to those who come after them a ruin instead of a habitation; and teaching their successors as little to respect their contrivances, as they had themselves respected the institutions of their forefathers. By this unprincipled facility of changing society as often, and as much, and in as many ways as there are floating fancies or fashions, the whole chain and continuity of the commonwealth would be broken. No one generation could link with the other. Men would become little better than the flies of summer.

18 *JOHN ADAMS* Today I was furnished with the fifteenth and sixteenth volumes of La Harpe's Course. They relate wholly to the philosophy of the eighteenth century. He distinguishes very justly between true and false philosophy. The latter is ascribed to the atheists and deists and in general all the enemies of religion whom he calls sophists. He goes over the productions of Condillac, Buffon, D'Alembert, Condorcet, Voltaire, Rousseau, Diderot, Boulanger, Raynal, and Mably, but these are but scraps. He makes Diderot the king of the sophists. He candidly allows them all their merits as fine writers but has no mercy on their absurdities, sophisms, hypocrisies, and lies. He ascribes the French Revolution to the sophists with all its horrors.

I have been delightfully entertained and much instructed by these books, and I think that any man who reads them with attention and impartiality must be convinced that the atheistic and deistic philosophers and their writings contributed a great deal to bring about the French Revolution, but especially to produce the worst parts, scenes, and most bloody horrors of it.

Piety and property, according to these profound philosophers, have been the sole causes of all the calamities and miseries of mankind. It seems to be almost a sin, as well as a folly, to reason with these great "masters of the depths." But I cannot help considering whether men were so happy according to the ideas of these gentlemen as to be totally destitute of the love, fear, and belief of a god—and to be agreed to have no property—whether they might not freeze in our cold winter night without houses to shelter them; whether they might not melt in the heats of summer; whether they or their children might not be unluckily torn by wild beasts; whether the old might not perish for want when their children had no faith in any precept to honor father and mother; and whether children would not suffer when their parents were sick or drunk with eating too many grapes or drinking too much of their juice.

[19] *JOHN ADAMS* I will give you a sample of Diderot's atheism, from La Harpe (volume 16, page 155): "He had become an atheist, to the point of going into rage at the name of God alone, and of regarding the idea of a God as the first of the scourges of the earth."

[20] *JOHN ADAMS* It must be confessed that this is much more profound than Rousseau's fable of the first man who marked or staked out a garden and called it his own. "This man ought to have been instantly put to death," as Rousseau says. And I say that both Rousseau and Diderot ought to have been sent to asylums. How it was possible that such knaves could associate with two or three

other knaves and find so many dupes, and among them princes, magistrates, nobles, philosophers, some of whom were respectable characters, I cannot conceive.

21 *DANIEL WEBSTER* I will go farther and say that this philosophy, this scheme or system, in its tendencies and effects, is opposed to all religions of every kind. 22 *JOHN ADAMS* The very scheme for the perfectibility of man to such a degree as to make laws unnecessary was not to be expected to be accomplished in less than thousands of years. This would, to my contracted mind, have been sufficient to discredit the philosophy forever!

23 *DAVID SWING* This philosophy is contrary to all the facts of history and experience; for while Hellenism, the very flower of human culture, was conscienceless, Hebraism and Christianity taught the supremacy of conscience. By appealing to and educating man's moral nature, Christianity has done more to elevate the world than all the acuteness of Greece, the power of Rome, or even the polish of modern Europe.

24 *M.H. CARPENTER* That Jesus, surrounded as He was, could have promulgated a system of morals embodying all that is most valuable in the prior life of the world, and to which nineteen centuries of civilization have not been able to add a thought or impart an ornament, is a fact not to be explained by any ridicule.

25 *DANIEL WEBSTER* Why should we shut our eyes to the whole history of Christianity? Is it not the preaching of ministers of the gospel that has evangelized the more civilized part of the world? Why do we, at this day, enjoy the lights and benefits of Christianity ourselves? And at what age of the Christian era have those who professed to teach the Christian religion, or to believe in its authority and importance, not insisted on the absolute necessity of inculcating

its principles and its precepts into the minds of the young? In what age, by what sect, where, when, and by whom, has religious truth been excluded from the education of youth? No where! Never! Everywhere and all times it has been, and it is, regarded as essential! It is the essence, the vitality, of useful instruction!

26 *DANIEL WEBSTER* If these reformers and philosophers would teach our children, what would become of their morals, their excellence, their purity of heart and life, their hope for time and eternity? What considerate man can enter a school and not reflect with awe that it is a seminary where immortal minds are training for eternity? What parent but is at times weighed down with the thought that there must be laid the foundations of a building which will stand, not merely when a temple or palace, but when the perpetual hills and adamantine† rocks on which they rest have melted away? 27 *DANIEL WEBSTER* What would be the condition of families, of children, if fathers and mothers were to teach their sons and daughters no religious tenets? 28 *DANIEL WEBSTER* What would become of all those thousand ties of sweetness, benevolence, love, and Christian feeling that now render our young men and young maidens like comely plants growing up by a streamlet's side—the graces and the grace of opening manhood and of blossoming womanhood? 29 *DANIEL WEBSTER* What is likely to be the effect of this system on the minds of children thus left solely to its pernicious influence with no one to care for their spiritual welfare in this world or the next? 30 *DANIEL WEBSTER* What would become of all that now renders the social circle lovely and beloved? What would become of society itself? How could it exist? 31 *DANIEL WEBSTER* Is that to be considered an education which strikes at the root of all this? Which subverts all the excellence and the charms of social

---

†   Adamantine: unbreakable, unyielding.

life? Which tends to destroy the very foundational framework of society, both in its practices and in its opinions? Which subverts the whole decency, the whole morality, as well as the whole Christianity and government of society? No, sir! No, sir!

[32] *DANIEL WEBSTER* Children left entirely to the tender mercies of those who will try upon them this experiment of moral philosophy or philosophical morality? [33] *DANIEL WEBSTER* Morality without sentiment, without benevolence towards man, without a sense of responsibility towards God, the duties of this life performed without any reference to the life which is to come: *this* is the reformer's theory of useful education? No, sir!

[34] *BENJAMIN RUSH* I say the great enemy of the salvation of man never invented a more effective means of limiting Christianity from the world than by persuading mankind that it was improper to read the Bible at schools! [35] *DANIEL WEBSTER* I say moral instruction, not resting on a Christian foundation, is only a building upon sand! [36] *GEORGE MASON* I say we must transmit to our posterity those sacred rights in which we ourselves were born!

[37] *THOMAS HODGSKIN* Men had better be without education than be educated by these reformers! Their education is but the mere breaking in of the steer to the yoke, the mere discipline of the hunting dog hastened to the feet of his master; [38] *BENJAMIN DISRAELI* the commencing of tyranny in the nursery! [39] *THOMAS JEFFERSON* If it is believed that elementary schools would be better managed by the governor and council or any other general authority of the government than by the parents within each ward, it is a belief against all experience! [40] *DANIEL WEBSTER* No, sir!

[41] *SAMUEL ADAMS* Let the principles of virtue be early inculcated on the minds of children and the moral sense kept alive. [42] *ALEXANDER REED*

Let the youth try to understand the world's mysteries; let them think much of its responsibilities; let them ponder the thoughts of the inquiring minds of all ages; let them prize all the light we have from man, from God, so that they may be guided aright amid its perils and changing experiences; 43 *PHILLIPS BROOKS* let them ever glory in something and strive to retain their admiration for all that would ennoble and their interest in all that would enrich and beautify their life!

44 *SAMUEL ADAMS* Our ancestors laid an excellent foundation for the security of liberty by setting up in a few years after their arrival a public seminary of learning; and by their laws, they obliged every town consisting of a certain number of families to keep and maintain a grammar school. In so doing, they impressed upon the minds of the people the necessity and importance of encouraging that system of education, which, in my opinion, is so well calculated to diffuse among the individuals of the community the principles of morality so essentially necessary to the preservation of public liberty.

45 *JAMES MONROE* Such an institution, which endeavors to rear American youth in pure love of truth and duty, while it enlightens their minds by ingenious and liberal studies, endeavors to awaken a love of country, soften local prejudices, and inculcate Christian faith and charity. Such an institution cannot but acquire, as it deserves, the confidence of the wise and good.

46 *BENJAMIN FRANKLIN* If men may, and frequently do, catch such a taste for cultivating flowers, for planting, grafting, inoculating and the like, as to despise all other amusements for their sake, why may not we expect they should acquire a relish for that more useful culture of young minds? 47 *BENJAMIN FRANKLIN* That such persons would apply for a charter by which they may be incorporated

with power to erect an academy for the education of youth, to govern the same, provide masters, make rules, receive donations, and purchase lands; *48 BENJAMIN FRANKLIN* that a house be provided for the academy, if not in the town, not many miles from it; the situation high and dry, and if it may be, not far from a river, having a garden, orchard, meadow, and a field or two; that the house be furnished with a library with maps of all countries, globes, some mathematical instruments, an apparatus for experiments in natural philosophy, and for mechanics; prints, of all kinds, prospects, buildings and machines;

49 BENJAMIN FRANKLIN that the rector be a person of good understanding, good morals, diligent and patient, learned in the languages and sciences, and a correct, pure speaker and writer of the English tongue;

50 BENJAMIN FRANKLIN that to keep them in health, and to strengthen and render active their bodies, they be frequently exercised in running, leaping, wrestling, and swimming;

51 BENJAMIN FRANKLIN that the teaching of history will afford frequent opportunities of showing the necessity of religion, from its usefulness to the publick; the advantage of a religious character among private persons; and the excellency of the Christian religion above all others ancient or modern;

52 BENJAMIN FRANKLIN that children be taught morality by descanting and making continual observations on the causes of the rise or fall of any man's character, fortune, and power; the advantages of temperance, order, frugality, industry, and perseverance; and to fix in the minds of youth deep impressions of the beauty and usefulness of virtue of all kinds, public spirit, and fortitude;

53 BENJAMIN FRANKLIN that questions of right and wrong, justice and injustice, be put to youth which they may debate in conversation and in writing;

54 *JOHN ADAMS* that in company with Sallust, Cicero, Tacitus, and Livy, they will learn wisdom and virtue; that they will see them represented with all the charms which language and imagination can exhibit and with vice and folly painted in all their deformity and horror;

55 *BENJAMIN FRANKLIN* that the idea of what is true merit should also be often presented to youth, explained and impressed on their minds as consisting in an inclination joined with an ability to serve mankind, one's country, friends, and family, which ability is—with the blessing of God—to be acquired or greatly increased by true learning, and should indeed be the great aim and end of all learning;

56 *THOMAS JEFFERSON* that youth would be enlightened by the mathematical and physical sciences which advance the arts and administer to the health, the subsistence, and comforts of human life;

57 *ALEXANDER HAMILTON* that property be taught as the basis of the freedom of the American yeomanry,[†] 58 *BENJAMIN FRANKLIN* along with the history of commerce, the invention of arts, the rise of manufactures, the progress of trade, the change of its seats with the reasons, causes, and consequences; that this may also be made entertaining to youth and useful to all;

59 *BENJAMIN FRANKLIN* that history will also give occasion to expatiate on the advantage of civil orders and constitutions, how men and their properties are protected by joining in societies and establishing government, their industry encouraged and rewarded,

---

[†] Yeomanry: the farming class; a body of middle class land owners.

arts invented, and life made more comfortable;

60 GEORGE WASHINGTON that the education of our youth in the science of government be a primary object: 61 BENJAMIN FRANKLIN the advantages of liberty, mischiefs of licentiousness, and benefits arising from good laws and a due execution of justice; and that the first principles of sound politics be fixed in the minds of youth.

62 JOHN ADAMS To what higher object, to what greater character, can any mortal aspire than to be possessed of all this knowledge, well-digested and ready at command, to assist the feeble and friendless, to discountenance the haughty and lawless, to procure redress to wrongs, the advancement of rights, to assert and maintain liberty and virtue, and to discourage and abolish tyranny and vice.

63 JOSEPH STORY Let the American youth never forget that they possess a noble inheritance, bought by the toils, sufferings, and blood of their ancestors, and that they have the capacity, if wisely improved and faithfully guarded, of transmitting to their posterity all the substantial blessings of life, the peaceful enjoyment of liberty, property, religion, and independence.

64 JOHN ADAMS My friends, instead of adoring a Washington, we should applaud the nation which educated him. I glory in the character of a Washington, because I know him to be only an exemplification of the American character.

Chapter Four
Rights

[1] *JOHN DICKINSON* Kings or parliaments could not give us the rights essential to happiness. Our rights are not annexed to us by parchments and seals. We claim them from a higher source—from the King of kings and Lord of all the earth. [2] *ALEXIS DE TOCQUEVILLE* For it was not man who implanted in himself what is infinite and the love of what is immortal; those lofty instincts are not the offspring of man's capricious will. Their steadfast foundation is fixed in our nature. [3] *JOHN DICKINSON* Our rights are created in us by the decrees of Providence. They are born with us; exist with us; and cannot be taken from us by any human power without taking our lives.

[4] *ALEXIS DE TOCQUEVILLE* I say rights, for such we have, undoubtedly, antecedent to all earthly government; rights that cannot be repealed or restrained by human laws; [5] *WILLIAM BLACKSTONE* rights that are binding over all the globe, in all countries, and at all times; the absolute rights of mankind as free agents, endowed with discernment to know good from evil, with the power of choosing those measures most desirable—this being one of the gifts of God to man at his creation, when He imbued man with the faculty of free will.

[6] *THOMAS JEFFERSON* As God has made it a law in the nature of man

to pursue his own happiness, He has left man free in the choice of place as well as mode; and we may safely call on all of history to produce the map on which Nature has traced—for each individual—the geographical line which she forbids him to cross in pursuit of happiness. But it certainly does not exist in his mind. Where then is it?

7 *THOMAS JEFFERSON* The evidence of natural right, like that of our right to life, liberty, the use of our faculties, and the pursuit of happiness, is not left to the feeble and sophistical investigations of reason, but is impressed on the sense of every man. 8 *OSWALD CHAMBERS* A man's conscience is the internal perception of God's moral law.

9 *JOHN LOCKE* The moral law obliges every one and teaches all mankind, that no one ought to harm another in his life, health, liberty, or possessions; 10 *RICHARD HOOKER* that a man's desire to be loved by his equals in nature imposes upon him a natural duty of bearing toward them fully the like affection; 11 *IMMANUEL KANT* that a man must bring the moral law to bear upon himself. 12 *MATTHEW 7:12* To do unto others as you would have others do unto you.

13 *THOMAS AQUINAS* All men are equal in nature, and also in original sin. 14 *THOMAS JEFFERSON* Hence envy and malice will never be quiet, 15 *MERCY OTIS WARREN* nor a man's propensity to tyrannize over his fellow men. The love of domination, the uncontrolled lust of arbitrary power— 16 *HUGO BLACK* these same kind of human evils have emerged from century to century, as excessive power is ever sought by the few at the expense of the many.

17 *THOMAS JEFFERSON* History, in general, only informs us of what bad government is. 18 *MICHEL GUILLAUME JEAN DE CRÈVECOEUR* It is the history of the earth: crimes of the most heinous nature, committed from

one end of the world to the other. We observe avarice, rapine,† and murder, equally prevailing in all parts. History perpetually tells us of millions of people abandoned to the caprice of the maddest princes and of whole nations devoted to the blind fury of tyrants. Countries destroyed; nations alternately buried in ruins by other nations; and the toil of thousands in a short time destroyed by a few.

[19] *JOHN LOCKE* The reason why a man enters into civil society is the preservation of his life and property. And the reason he chooses and authorizes a legislature is that there may be laws made and rules set as guards and fences—to the lives and properties of all the members of the society—to limit the power and moderate the dominion of every part and member of the society. [20] *WILLIAM BLACKSTONE* For no man who considers a moment would wish to retain the absolute and uncontrolled power of doing whatever he pleases—the consequence of which is that every other man would also have the same power, and then there would be no security to individuals in any of the enjoyments of life.

[21] *SAMUEL ADAMS* When a man enters into civil society, it is by voluntary consent, and he has a right to demand and insist upon the performance of such conditions and previous limitations as form an equitable original compact. [22] *RICHARD HENRY LEE* He does not resign all his rights to those who govern, but he does fix limits to the legislators and rulers. [23] *JOHN LOCKE* For he cannot delegate to government the power to do anything to another person which would be unlawful for him to do himself.

[24] *THOMAS JEFFERSON* Sadly, our legislators are not sufficiently apprised of the rightful limits of their power, that their true office is to

---

†   Seizure of someone's property.

declare and enforce only our natural rights and duties; to take none of them from us; 25 *JAMES MADISON* to guard a man's house as his castle; to pay public and enforce private debts with the most exact faith; to scrupulously guard the possessions of individuals; to protect them in the enjoyment and communication of their opinions; 26 *JAMES MADISON* and to give no title to invade a man's conscience.

27 *SAMUEL ADAMS* My fellow citizens, it is the greatest absurdity to suppose it in the power of a man, at the entering into society, to renounce his essential rights, or the means of preserving those rights, when the grand end of civil government from the very nature of its institution, is for the support, protection, and defense of those rights! 28 *JAMES MADISON* For that is not a just government, nor is property secure under it, where the property which a man has in his personal safety and personal liberty, is violated by arbitrary seizures of one class of citizens for the service of the rest!

29 *JAMES MADISON* Citizens! Charity is no part of the legislative duty of the government! 30 *ALEXIS DE TOCQUEVILLE* The Constitution is not an endlessly expanding list of rights—the "right" to education, the "right" to healthcare, the "right" to food and housing. Those aren't rights; those are the rations of slavery—hay and a barn for human cattle. That's not freedom! That's dependency!

31 *JAMES MADISON* To take the words "general welfare" in a literal and unlimited sense is a metamorphosis of the Constitution into a character which there is a host of proofs was not contemplated by its creators! 32 *EDMUND BURKE* Every wanton law, every causeless restraint of the will of the subject, whether practiced by a monarch, a nobility, or a popular assembly, is a degree of tyranny! Nay, that even laws themselves—whether made with or without our consent, if they regulate and constrain conduct in matters of mere indifference, without any good end in view—are laws

destructive of liberty!

33 *HERBERT SPENCER* What do we want a government for? Not to educate the people; not to teach religion, not to administer charity; not to make railways; but simply to defend the natural rights of man; to protect person and property; to prevent the aggressions of the powerful upon the weak; in a word, to administer justice. This is the natural, original office of civil government. It was not intended to do less; it ought not to be allowed to do more!

34 *THOMAS JEFFERSON* No man has a natural right to commit aggression on the equal rights of another, and this is all from which the laws ought to restrict him! Every man is under the natural duty of contributing to the necessities of society, and this is all the laws should enforce on him!

35 *JAMES MADISON* The legislative has no right to absolute, arbitrary power over the lives and fortunes of the people! 36 *LYSANDER SPOONER* A man's natural rights are his own—against the whole world! And any infringement of them is a crime, whether committed by one man calling himself a robber, or by millions calling themselves a government!!!

37 *JOSIAH QUINCY* Who are the persons to whom such unbounded enormous power is entrusted? 38 *THOMAS PAINE* Rights are not gifts from one man to another, nor from one class of men to another; for who is he who could be the first giver, or by what principle, or on what authority could he possess the right given?

39 *GAD HITCHCOCK* My friends, it is altogether unreasonable to suppose a number of persons, by a free and voluntary contract, should give up themselves, their families, and estates so absolutely into the hands of any rulers, as not to make a reserve of the right of saving themselves from ruin; and if they should, the bargain

would be void, as counteracting the will of Heaven and the powerful law of self-preservation. For it must be granted that the people have a right in some circumstances, or that they have not a right in any, to oppose their rulers—there is no medium.

40 *GAD HITCHCOCK* If it be true that no rulers can be safe where the doctrine of resistance is taught, then it must be true that no nation can be safe where the contrary is taught: If it be true that this disposeth men of turbulent spirits to oppose the best rulers, it is as true that the other disposeth princes of evil minds to enslave and ruin the best and most submissive subjects. If it be true that this encourageth all public disturbance, and all revolutions whatsoever, it is as true that the other encourageth all tyranny and all the most intolerable persecutions and oppressions imaginable. And on which side then will the advantage lie? And which of the two shall we choose for the sake of the happy effects and consequences of it?

With respect, therefore, to rulers of evil dispositions, nothing is more necessary than that they should believe resistance in some cases to be lawful—not for a few discontented individuals who may happen to take it into their heads to resist, but for the majority of a community, either by themselves or through their representatives, to resist.

41 *GAD HITCHCOCK* Many rulers, indeed, cannot bear the propagation of this doctrine; but the reason why they cannot is, namely, its being preventive of their pernicious designs, which is an undeniable argument of its being the more necessary!

42 *GEORGE TUCKER* My fellow citizens, the right of self-defense is the true palladium of liberty! 43 *FRÉDÉRIC BASTIAT* Each of us has a natural right from God to defend his person, his liberty, and his property!

[44] *JOHN LOCKE* It is the right of a man to punish the transgressors of law to such a degree as may hinder its violation—to preserve the innocent, and restrain the offenders! [45] *AUGUSTINE OF HIPPO* For though defensive violence will always be "a sad necessity" in the eyes of men of principle, it would be still more unfortunate if wrongdoers should dominate just men!

[46] *TENCH COXE* Let it be known that the unlimited power of the sword is not in the hands of either the federal or state governments, but—where I trust in God it will ever remain—in the hands of the people! [47] *JAMES MADISON* Let it be known that a people armed and free, forms a barrier against the enterprises of ambition—a bulwark for this nation against foreign invasion and domestic oppression! [48] *JOHN ADAMS* Let it be known that the right of a nation to kill a tyrant, in cases of necessity, can no more be doubted than to hang a robber or kill a flea!!!

[49] *JOHN ADAMS* Yet killing one tyrant, my friends, only makes way for a worse, unless the people have sense, spirit, and honesty enough to establish and support a constitution guarded at all points against tyranny—against the tyranny of the one, the few, and the many.

[50] *THOMAS PAINE* A constitution is not the act of a government, but of a people constituting a government; and government without a constitution, is power without a right. [51] *THOMAS PAINE* For all power exercised over a nation must have some beginning. It must either be delegated or assumed. There are no other sources. All delegated power is trust, and all assumed power is usurpation. Time does not alter the nature and quality of either.

[52] *ALEXANDER HAMILTON* This important distinction so well understood in America—between a constitution established by the people and unalterable by the government, and a law established by the

government and alterable by the government—seems to have been little understood and less observed in any other country.

53 *NOAH WEBSTER* Every person moderately acquainted with human nature knows that public bodies, as well as individuals, are liable to the influence of sudden and violent passions under the operation of which the voice of reason is silenced. 54 *JOSEPH STORY* Temporary delusions, prejudices, excitements, and objects have irresistible influence in mere questions of policy. 55 *JOSEPH STORY* A constitution is not subject to such fluctuations. It is to have a fixed, uniform, permanent construction. It should be, so far at least as human infirmity will allow, not dependent upon the passions or parties of particular times, but the same yesterday, today, and forever.

56 *THOMAS JEFFERSON* The purpose of a written constitution is to bind up the several branches of government by certain laws, which, when they transgress, their acts shall become nullities; to render unnecessary an appeal to the people, or in other words a rebellion, on every infraction of their rights. 57 *DANIEL WEBSTER* For we may be tossed upon an ocean where we can see no land—not, perhaps, the sun or stars. But there is a chart and a compass for us to study, to consult, and to obey. The chart is the Constitution.

58 *DANIEL WEBSTER* Every man's heart swells within him; every man's port and bearing becomes somewhat more proud and lofty as he remembers that this great inheritance of liberty is still his; his, undiminished and unimpaired; his, in all its original glory; his to enjoy; his to protect; and his to transmit to future generations.

59 *GEORGE WASHINGTON* The Constitution—the offspring of our own choice, uninfluenced and unawed, adopted upon full investigation and mature deliberation, completely free in its principles,

in the distribution of its powers, uniting security with energy, and containing within itself a provision for its own amendment—has a just claim to your confidence and your support. 60 GEORGE WASHINGTON Until changed by an explicit and authentic act of the whole people, the Constitution is sacredly obligatory upon all. There must be no change by usurpation; for though this, in one instance, may be the instrument of good, it is the customary weapon by which free governments are destroyed.

61 GEORGE WASHINGTON The basis of our political systems is the right of the people to make and to alter their constitutions of government; 62 THOMAS JEFFERSON that the people may exercise this power by themselves, in all cases to which they think themselves competent, or they may act by representatives, freely and equally chosen; 63 EDMUND PENDLETON that the people's representatives may assemble in convention when necessary and wholly recall the delegated powers, or reform them so as to prevent abuse, and punish those servants who have perverted those powers.

64 GEORGE WASHINGTON If, in the opinion of the people, the distribution or modification of the constitutional powers be in any particular wrong, it can be corrected by an amendment in the way which the Constitution designates. That 65 CONSTITUTION ARTICLE V Congress, whenever two thirds of both Houses shall deem it necessary, shall propose amendments to this Constitution, or, on the application of the legislatures of two thirds of the several states, shall call a convention for proposing amendments, which, in either case, shall be valid to all intents and purposes, as part of this Constitution, when ratified by the legislatures of three fourths of the several states, or by conventions in three fourths thereof, as the one or the other mode of ratification may be proposed by the Congress.

66 THOMAS JEFFERSON This example of changing a constitution by

assembling the people of the state, instead of assembling armies, will be worth as much to the world as the former examples we had given them. 67 *JOSEPH STORY* But if the people do not choose to apply this remedy, it may fairly be presumed that the mischief is less than what would arise from a further extension of the power; or that it is the least of two evils.

68 *THOMAS JEFFERSON* On every question of construction of the Constitution, let us carry ourselves back to the time when the Constitution was adopted; let us recollect the spirit of the debates, and instead of trying what meaning may be squeezed out of the text or invented against it, conform to the probable one in which it was passed. 69 *DANIEL WEBSTER* For if an angel should be winged from heaven on an errand of mercy to our country, the first accents that would glow on his lips would be, "Beware! Be cautious! You have everything to lose and nothing to gain." We live under the only government that ever existed which was framed by the unrestrained and deliberate consultations of the people. Miracles do not cluster. That which has happened but once in six thousand years cannot be expected to happen often. Such a government, once gone, might leave a void to be filled for ages with revolution and tumult, riot and despotism.

70 *JOHN PHILPOT CURRAN* My friends, the condition upon which God hath given liberty to man is eternal vigilance, which condition if he breaks, servitude is at once the consequence of his crime and the punishment of his guilt. 71 *ALEXIS DE TOCQUEVILLE* True friends of liberty ought constantly to be on the alert to prevent the power of government from lightly sacrificing the private rights of individuals, 72 *JAMES MADISON* to take alarm at the first experiment on their liberties. We hold this prudent jealousy to be the first duty of citizens.

73 JAMES MADISON The people of the United States owe their independence and their liberty to the wisdom of descrying,† in the minute a tax of three pence on tea, the magnitude of the evil comprised in the precedent. Let them exert the same wisdom in watching against every evil lurking under plausible disguises and growing up from small beginnings. *74 ALEXIS DE TOCQUEVILLE* For no citizen is so obscure that it is not very dangerous to allow him to be oppressed; no private rights are so unimportant that they can be surrendered with impunity to the caprices of government.

75 GAD HITCHCOCK Our danger is not visionary, but real. Our contention is not about trifles but about liberty and property, and not ours only, but those of posterity to the latest generations. Every lover of mankind will allow that these are important objects, too inestimably precious and valuable enjoyments to be treated with neglect and tamely surrendered; for however some few, I speak it with regret and astonishment, even from among ourselves, appear sufficiently disposed to ridicule the rights of America and the liberties of its people. 'Tis plain St. Paul, who was a good judge, had a very different sense of them: "He was on all occasions for standing fast, not only in the liberties with which Christ had made him free from the Jewish law of ceremonies, but also in that liberty with which the laws of nature had made him free from oppression and tyranny."

76 GAD HITCHCOCK If I am mistaken in supposing plans are formed and executed, subversive of our natural and charter rights and privileges and incompatible with every idea of liberty, all America is mistaken with me.

77 GAD HITCHCOCK The united voice of America, with the solemnity of

---

† Descrying: revealing.

thunder and with piercings of lightning, awakes your attention and demands fidelity. [78] *JAMES MADISON* The free men of America did not wait until usurped power had strengthened itself by exercise. They saw all the consequences in the principle, and they avoided the consequences by denying the principle.

[79] *DANIEL WEBSTER* We, too, are bound to maintain public liberty and, by the example of our own systems, to convince the world that order and law, religion and morality, the rights of conscience, the rights of persons, and the rights of property, may all be preserved and secured in the most perfect manner by a government entirely and purely elective.

[80] *DANIEL WEBSTER* If we fail in this, our disaster will be significant. [81] *THOMAS JEFFERSON* Our rulers will become corrupt; our people, careless. The people will be forgotten, therefore, and their rights disregarded. They will forget themselves but in the sole faculty of making money and will never think of uniting to affect a due respect for their rights. The shackles, therefore, will be made heavier and heavier, until our rights shall revive, or expire in a convulsion.

Chapter Five
Tyrants

1 *SAMUEL ADAMS* The time may come when all will be reversed; when our excellent Constitution of government will be subverted; when we are pressed by debts and taxes; when the influence of the crown, strengthened by luxury and a universal profligacy of manners will have tainted every heart, broken down every fence of liberty, and rendered us a nation of tame and contented vassals; when a general election will be nothing but a general auction of boroughs; and when the parliament will be degenerated into a body of sycophants, dependent and venal, always ready to confirm any measures, and little more than a public court for registering royal edicts.

2 *SAMUEL ADAMS* What will, at that period, be the duty of the colonies? Will they be still bound to unconditional submission? Must they always continue an appendage to our government and follow it implicitly through every change that can happen to it? Wretched condition, indeed, of millions of freemen as good as ourselves! Will you say that we are now governed equitably and that there is no danger of such revolution? Would to God that this were true! Who shall judge whether we are governed equitably or not? Can you give the colonies any security that such a period will never come? No. The period, countrymen, is already come!

TYRANTS

[3] *THOMAS JEFFERSON* Our government is now taking so steady a course as to show by what road it will pass to destruction—to wit, by consolidation first, and then corruption. The engine of consolidation will be the federal judiciary—the two other branches, the corrupting and corrupted instruments, [4] *JOHN DICKINSON* as our government hardens into a tyrannical monopoly, and the human race in general become as absolute property, as beasts in the plow.

[5] *JONATHAN MAYHEW* Those nations that are now groaning under the iron scepter of tyranny were once free. So they might probably have remained by seasonable caution against despotic measures. For civil tyranny is usually small in its beginning. The evil comes as "the drop of a bucket" until at length, like a mighty torrent or the raging waves of the sea, it bears down all before it and deluges whole countries and empires.

[6] *EDMUND BURKE* Liberty is nibbled away for expedience, and by parts; [7] *HILAIRE BELLOC* sumptuary laws on food and drink, conscription, a cast-iron system of compulsory instruction for all, [8] *THOMAS JEFFERSON* growth and entailment of a public debt, the multiplication of public offices, covering the land with officers, and opening our doors to their intrusions. Such is the process of domiciliary vexation which, once entered, is scarcely to be restrained from reaching successively every article of produce and property.

[9] *JOHN LOCKE* What is tyranny? While usurpation is the exercise of power, which another hath a right to; tyranny is the exercise of power beyond right, which no body can have a right to. And this is making use of the power any one has in his hands, not for the good of those who are under it, but for his own private separate advantage. When the governor, however entitled, makes not the law, but his will, the rule; and his commands and actions are not directed to the preservation of the properties of his people, but

the satisfaction of his own ambition, revenge, covetousness, or any other irregular passion, there you have tyranny.

10 *THOMAS PAINE* The greatest tyrannies are always perpetuated in the name of the noblest causes. 11 *JOHN ADAMS* Power always thinks that it is doing God's service when it is violating all His laws. 12 *JOSIAH QUINCY* There are men who must support their dignity by the assistance of the worthless and wicked; 13 *CESARE BECCARIA* men who had rather command the sentiments of mankind than excite them; 14 *ALEXANDER HAMILTON* men of factious tempers, of local prejudices, of sinister designs, who then, by intrigue, by corruption, or by other means, betray the interests of the people.

15 *CICERO* A nation can survive its fools, and even the ambitious. But it cannot survive treason from within. An enemy at the gates is less formidable for he is known and carries his banner openly. But the traitor moves amongst those within the gate freely, his sly whispers rustling through all the alleys, heard in the very halls of government itself—16 *ALEXANDER HAMILTON* an avaricious man who betrays the interests of the state for the acquisition of wealth; an ambitious man who makes his own aggrandizement through the aid of a foreign power.

17 *CICERO* The traitor appears not a traitor; he speaks in accents familiar to his victims, and he wears their face and their arguments. He appeals to the baseness that lies deep in the hearts of all men. He rots the soul of a nation; he works secretly and unknown in the night to undermine the pillars of the city; he infects the body politic so that it can no longer resist. A murderer is less to fear. The traitor is the plague!

18 *CONSTITUTION ARTICLE III* Treason against the United States consists only in levying war against them, or in adhering to their enemies,

giving them aid and comfort. [19] *US CODE 18-2381* Whoever is guilty of treason shall suffer death or shall be imprisoned not less than five years and fined under this title but not less than $10,000; and shall be incapable of holding any office under the United States. [20] *GEORGE WASHINGTON* For no punishment, in my opinion, is too great for the man who can build his greatness upon his country's ruin!

[21] *GEORGE WASHINGTON* How our enemies, despairing of carrying the point by force, are practicing every base art to effect by bribery and corruption what they cannot accomplish in a manly way. [22] *GEORGE WASHINGTON* How pitiful, in the eye of reason and religion, is this false ambition which desolates the world with fire and sword for the purposes of conquest and fame. [23] *GEORGE WASHINGTON* How easily is arbitrary power established on the ruins of liberty abused to licentiousness.

[24] *SAMUEL ADAMS* It is in the interest of tyrants to reduce the people to ignorance and vice; to destroy the people's liberties; to poison their morals; to employ every art to sooth the devoted people into a state of indolence and inattention. [25] *THOMAS JEFFERSON* For as the passions of men will take their course, they will not be controlled but by despotism, and this melancholy truth is the pretext for despotism.

[26] *ALEXIS DE TOCQUEVILLE* Society is not endangered only by the great profligacy of a few, but by the laxity of morals amongst all. When the taste for physical gratifications among the people has grown more rapidly than their education; when men are carried away and lose all self-restraint; [27] *FRÉDÉRIC BASTIAT* when misguided public opinion honors what is despicable and despises what is honorable, punishes virtue and rewards vice, encourages what is harmful and discourages what is useful, applauds falsehood and smothers truth under indifference or insult; [28] *ALEXIS DE TOCQUEVILLE*

then it is not necessary to do violence to such a people in order to strip them of the rights they enjoy. They themselves willingly loosen their hold. They neglect their chief business, which is to remain their own masters.

29 *JOHN ADAMS* A master requires of all who seek his favor an implicit resignation to his will and humor, and these require that he be soothed, flattered, and assisted in his vices and follies, perhaps the blackest crimes that men can commit. The first thought of this will produce in a mind a soliloquy, as if he should say, "The minister of state or the governor would promote my interest, would advance me to places of honor and profit, would raise me to titles and dignities that will be perpetuated in my family—in a word, would make the fortune of me and my posterity forever if I would but comply with his desires and become his instrument to promote his measures. He requires of me such compliances, such horrid crimes, such a sacrifice of my honor, my conscience, my friends, my country, my God, as the Scriptures inform us must be punished with nothing less than hellfire, eternal torment. If I could but deceive myself so far as to think eternity a moment only, I could comply and be promoted."

30 *JOHN ADAMS* In this, the charms of wealth and power are so enchanting, and the belief of future punishments so faint, that men find ways to persuade themselves to believe any absurdity— to submit to any prostitution—rather than forgo their wishes and desires. Their imaginations are so strong and their reason so weak, and, at last, their reason serves as an eloquent advocate on the side of their passions as they bring themselves to believe that black is white, that vice is virtue, that folly is wisdom, and that eternity is but a moment.

31 *MATTHEW 4:8–10* And thus the devil took Jesus up on an exceedingly

high mountain, and showed Him all the kingdoms of the world and their glory. And he said to Him, "All these things I will give You if You will fall down and worship me."

Then Jesus said to him, "Away with you, Satan! For it is written, 'You shall worship the Lord your God, and Him only you shall serve.'"

32 *ROMANS 1:21* Yet they neither glorified Him as God nor gave thanks to Him, but they became futile in their thinking and darkened in their foolish hearts. Although they claimed to be wise, they became fools, and exchanged the glory of the immortal God for images of mortal man and birds and animals and reptiles.

33 *GOUVERNEUR MORRIS* The literati, whose heads are turned by romantic notions picked up in books and who are too lofty to look down upon that kind of man which really exists and too wise to heed the dictates of common sense and experience, have turned the heads of their countrymen and have run amok with a Don Quixote constitution.

34 *THOMAS PAINE* The world they act in differs so materially from the world at large, that they have but little opportunity of knowing its true interests. 35 *THOMAS JEFFERSON* The moment these learned men form a theory, their imagination sees in every object only the traits which favor that theory.

SCRIBE When the Illuminati began recruiting in America, President Washington spoke out: 36 *GEORGE WASHINGTON* It is not my intention to doubt that the diabolical tenets of the Illuminati and the pernicious principles of the Jacobins has spread in the United States. On the contrary, no one is more satisfied of this fact than I am. That individuals of them may have done it, or that they may have had these objects and actually had a separation of the people from their government in view, is too evident to be questioned.

[37] *TIMOTHY DWIGHT* About the year 1728, Voltaire, so celebrated for his wit and brilliancy, and not less distinguished for his hatred of Christianity and his abandonment of principle, formed a systematical design to destroy Christianity and to introduce in its stead a general diffusion of irreligion and atheism. Doctrines were taught which strike at the root of all human happiness and virtue:

The being of God was denied and ridiculed.

Government was asserted to be a mere usurpation.

Civil society was declared to be the only apostasy of man.

The possession of property was pronounced to be robbery.

Chastity and natural affection were declared to be nothing more than groundless prejudices.

Adultery, assassination, poisoning, and other crimes of the like infernal nature, were taught as lawful, and even as virtuous actions.

To crown such a system of falsehood and horror all means were declared to be lawful, provided the end was good.

In this last doctrine, men are not only loosed from every bond and from every duty, but from every inducement to perform any thing which is good and abstain from any thing which is evil, and are set upon each other like a company of hellhounds to worry, rend, and destroy. Of the goodness of the end every man is to judge for himself; and most men pronounce every end to be good which will gratify their inclinations.

[38] *TIMOTHY DWIGHT* To accomplish their ends the ardor of innovation,

the impatience of civil and moral restraints, and the aims against government, morals, and religion, were elevated, expanded, and rendered more systematical, malignant, and daring. With unremitted ardor and diligence, the members insinuated themselves into every place of power and trust and into every literary, political, and friendly society. They engrossed as much as possible the education of youth; they became licensers of the press and directors of every literary journal; they waylaid every foolish prince, every unprincipled civil officer, and every abandoned clergyman; and with unhallowed hands and satanic lips, they polluted the pages of God.

[39] *TIMOTHY DWIGHT* Through sophistry—in which with great art and insidiousness the doctrines and teaching of history, as well as Christian theology, were rendered absurd and ridiculous, and the minds of men were insensibly steeled against conviction and duty—they designed to hold out themselves and their friends, as the only persons of great literary and intellectual distinction in order to dictate all opinions to the nation.

[40] *JOHN ADAMS* My friends, is there a possibility that the government of nations may fall into the hands of such men? Men who teach the most disconsolate of all creeds? That men are but fireflies? That all of creation is without a Father? Is this the way to make man, as man, an object of respect? Or is it to make murder itself as indifferent as shooting a plover† and the extermination of a nation as innocent as the swallowing of mites on a morsel of cheese? A certain duchess of venerable years and understanding, said of some of the philosophers of the eighteenth century, "On ne croit pas dans le Christianisme, mais on croit toutes les sottises

---

† Group of wading birds.

possibles;" that is, "They don't believe in Christianity, but they believe in every possible nonsense."

41 *ALEXIS DE TOCQUEVILLE* Has man always inhabited a world like the present, where nothing is linked together, where virtue is without genius, and genius without honor? Where the love of order is confounded with a taste for oppression, and the holy rites of freedom with a contempt of law? Where the light thrown by conscience on human actions is dim, and where nothing seems to be any longer forbidden or allowed, honorable or shameful, false or true?

42 *FRÉDÉRIC BASTIAT* You who wish to reform everything; you who judge humanity to be so small; 43 *JONATHAN EDWARDS* you who trust in your own righteousness, you arrogate to yourselves the honor of the greatest thing that even God Himself ever did! You seem not only sufficient to perform divine works, but such is your pride and vanity, you are not content without taking upon yourself to do the very greatest work that ever God Himself wrought: to take on yourself to work out the redemption of man!

44 *AUBERON HERBERT* Why should you desire to compel others? Why should you seek to have power—that evil, bitter, mocking thing, which has been from of old, as it is today, the sorrow and curse of the world—over your fellow men and fellow women? Why should you desire to take from any man or woman their own will and intelligence, their free choice, their own self-guidance, their inalienable rights over themselves? Why should you desire to make of them mere tools and instruments for your own advantage and interest? Why should you desire to compel them to serve and follow your opinions instead of their own? Why should you deny in them the soul that suffers so deeply from all constraints, and treat them as a sheet of blank paper upon which

you may write your own will and desires, of whatever kind they may happen to be? Who gave you the right? From where do you pretend to have received it, to degrade other men and women from their own true rank as human beings, taking from them their will, their conscience, and intelligence—in a word, all the best and highest part of their nature, turning them into mere empty worthless shells, mere shadows of true men and women, mere counters in the game you are mad enough to play, and just because you are more numerous or stronger than they, to treat them as if they belonged not to themselves, but to you? Can you believe that good will ever comes by morally and spiritually degrading your fellow men? What happy and safe and permanent form of society can you hope to build on this pitiful plan of subjecting others, or being yourselves subjected by them?

45 *FRÉDÉRIC BASTIAT* Oh, sublime writers! Remember that God has given to men all that is necessary for them to accomplish their destinies. Remember that humans are so constituted that they will develop themselves harmoniously in the clean air of liberty! Remember that this clay, this sand, and this manure which you so arbitrarily dispose of, are men! They are your equals! They are intelligent and free human beings like yourselves! As you have, they too have received from God the faculty to observe, to plan ahead, to think, and to judge for themselves!!!

46 *SAMUEL ADAMS* Were the talents and virtues which Heaven has bestowed on men given merely to make them mere obedient drudges to be sacrificed to the follies and ambition of a few? Or were not the noble gifts so equally dispensed with a divine purpose and law, that they should as nearly as possible be equally exerted and the blessings of providence be equally enjoyed by all? 47 *FREDERICK DOUGLASS* For I know no class of my fellowmen,

however just, enlightened, and humane, which can be wisely and safely trusted absolutely with the liberties of any other class!

48 *FRÉDÉRIC BASTIAT* Away, then, with the quacks and organizers! Away with their rings, chains, hooks, and pincers!† Away with their artificial systems! Away with the whims of governmental administrators, their socialized projects, their centralization, their tariffs, their government schools, their bank monopolies, their regulations, their restrictions, their equalization by taxation, and their pious moralizations!

49 *FRÉDÉRIC BASTIAT* And now that you legislators and do-gooders have so futilely inflicted so many systems upon mankind, may you finally end where you should have begun: May you try liberty, for liberty is an acknowledgment of faith in God and His works!

50 *ROMANS 1:20* Since the creation of the world God's invisible qualities—his eternal power and divine nature—have been clearly seen, being understood from what has been made, so that people are without excuse. 51 *JOHN OWEN* Yet man erects the idol of self; and not only wishes others to worship, but worships himself.

52 *D.L. MOODY* You can always tell when a man is a great ways from God. He is always talking about himself, how good he is. But the moment he sees God by the eye of faith, he is down on his knees, and, like Job, he cries, "Behold, I am vile!" 53 *ROMANS 7:19* For I do not that good thing that I will, but I do that evil thing that I will not. 54 *2 CORINTHIANS 12:9* And the Lord says to him, "My grace is sufficient for you, for my power is made perfect in weakness." 55 *MATTHEW 11:28-29* "Come unto me, all ye that labor and are heavy laden, and I will give you rest. Take my yoke upon you, and learn

---

† An instrument with a grasping jaw used for gripping things.

of me; for I am meek and lowly in heart: and ye shall find rest unto your souls."

56 *GOUVERNEUR MORRIS* The reflection and experience of many years have led me to consider the holy Writings not only as the most authentic and instructive in themselves, but as the clue to all other history. They tell us what man is, and they alone tell us why he is what he is: a contradictory creature that seeing and approving of what is good, pursues and performs what is evil. All of private and public life is there displayed. From the same pure fountain of wisdom, we learn that vice destroys freedom and that arbitrary power is founded on public immorality.

57 *SAMUEL ADAMS* My friends, the religion and public liberty of a people are intimately connected; their interests are interwoven. They cannot subsist separately; and therefore, they rise and fall together. 58 *GIROLAMO SAVONAROLA* Do you wish to be free? Then above all things, love God, love your neighbor, love one another, and love the common good. Then you will have true liberty. 59 *GEORGE M. ROBESON* For when men are brought into harmony with great ideas, striving for great ends; when the human heart, developing the germ of its immortal nature, rises to the height of the loftiest ideas, and enlarges to the compass of the broadest principles; 60 *HENRY WARD BEECHER* when we make men large and strong, tyranny will bankrupt itself in making shackles for them.

Chapter Six
Insurrection

1 *MONTESQUIEU* There is no crueler tyranny than that which is perpetuated under the shield of law and in the name of justice. 2 *JOHN LOCKE* Wherever the power that is put in any hands—for the government of the people and the preservation of their properties—is applied to other ends, and made use of to impoverish, harass, or subdue them to arbitrary and irregular commands, there it presently becomes tyranny, whether those that thus use it are one or many.

3 *THOMAS JEFFERSON* Law is often but the tyrant's will, and always so when it violates the right of an individual. 4 *FRÉDÉRIC BASTIAT* The law perverted; the law—and, in its wake, all the collective forces of the nation—the law, I say, not only diverted from its proper direction, but made to pursue one entirely contrary; the law becomes the tool of every kind of avarice instead of being its check. The law becomes guilty of that very iniquity which it was its mission to punish.

5 *THOMAS JEFFERSON* The most sacred of the duties of a government is to do equal and impartial justice to all its citizens. 6 *JONATHAN MAYHEW* The king is as much bound by his oath not to infringe on the legal rights of the people, as the people are bound to yield subjection to him. From whence it follows, that as soon as the prince

sets himself up above law, he loses the king in the tyrant. He does, to all intents and purposes, unking himself by acting out of, and beyond, that sphere which the constitution allows him to move in. And in such cases, he has no more right to be obeyed, than any inferior officer who acts beyond his commission. The subject's obligation to allegiance then ceases, of course; and to resist him is no more rebellion than to resist any foreign invader.

[7] *JOSEPH WARREN* Our laws seem to lie prostrate at the foot of power. Our city is yet a garrison filled with armed men, as our harbor is with cruisers, cutters, and other armed vessels. A main guard is yet placed at the doors of our state house. The other side of the exchange is turned into a guarded den of revenue officers to plunder our trade and drain the country of its money, not only without our consent, but against repeated remonstrances. The military are guilty of all kinds of licentiousness. The public streets are unsafe to walk in for either sex, by night or by day. Prosecutions, civil and criminal against the inhabitants, are pushed with great rancor and rigor. When every thing else fails, power is claimed as an uncontrollable prerogative of the Crown and, without exaggeration, this is the present wretched state of the once happy and flourishing city of Boston. Such in a degree is the state of all our trading towns, and such in effect is the state of the whole continent.

[8] *JOHN ADAMS* The year 1765 has been the most remarkable year of my life. That enormous engine, fabricated by the British Parliament, for battering down all the rights and liberties of America—I mean the Stamp Act—has raised and spread through the whole continent a spirit that will be recorded to our honor with all future generations.

In every colony, from Georgia to New Hampshire inclusively, the stamp distributors and inspectors have been compelled, by the unconquerable rage of the people, to renounce their offices. Such and so universal has been the resentment of the people that every man who has dared to speak in favor of the stamps, how great soever his abilities and virtues had been esteemed before, or whatever his fortune, connections, and influence had been, has been seen to sink into universal contempt and ignominy.

The people, even to the lowest ranks, have become more attentive to their liberties, more inquisitive about them, and more determined to defend them, than they were ever before known or had occasion to be. Innumerable have been the monuments of wit, humor, sense, learning, spirit, patriotism, and heroism, erected in the several colonies and provinces in the course of this year. Our presses have groaned, our pulpits have thundered, our legislatures have resolved, our towns have voted, the Crown's officers have everywhere trembled, and all their little tools and creatures have been afraid to speak and ashamed to be seen.

9 *JOHN DICKINSON BROADBOARD* Patriots, what steps you now take, without injury to our sacred rights, demands your maturest deliberation. If you comply with the Act by using stamped papers, you fix—you rivet—perpetual chains upon your unhappy country. You unnecessarily, voluntarily establish the detestable precedent which those who have forged your fetters ardently wish for, to varnish the future exercise of this new-claimed authority.

The Stamp Act is to be regarded only as an experiment of your disposition. If you quietly bend your necks to that yoke, you prove yourselves ready to receive any bondage to which your lords and masters shall please to subject you. Can we imagine, then, that Parliament will consent to pass an Act to renounce this advantage? No! Power is of a tenacious nature: What it seizes, it will retain. Rouse yourselves, therefore, my dear countrymen.

Think, oh! Think of the endless miseries you must entail upon yourselves and your country by touching the pestilential cargoes that have been sent to you. Destruction lurks within them. To receive them is death! No! It is worse than death, it is *slavery*!

SCRIBE In Boston, nine merchants, tradesmen, and seamen organized to stand up to the tyranny of the Stamp Act. The names of these Loyal Nine must never be forgotten:

~ John Avery, distiller; club secretary
~ Henry Bass, jeweler and cousin of Samuel Adams
~ Thomas Chase, distiller
~ Steven Cleverly, brazier (metal craftsman)
~ Thomas Crafts, painter
~ Benjamin Edes, printer of the Boston Gazette and friend of Samuel Adams
~ Joseph Field, ship captain
~ John Smith, brazier
~ George Trott, jeweler

SCRIBE The Loyal Nine soon became known as the Sons of Liberty, patriot groups that began to form across the Colonies.

[10] *SAMUEL ADAMS* The Sons of Liberty, on the 14th of August, 1765—a day which ought to be forever remembered in America—animated with a zeal for their country then upon the brink of destruction, resolved at once to save her. [11] *JOHN BOYLE* Patriots prepared effigies of Andrew Oliver, the Stamp Master, and Lord Bute, the king's favorite, who was considered the instigator of the unpopular revenue measures. The Sons of Liberty then hung the effigies from a large elm tree at Essex and Orange Streets in the South End, a tree soon to become famous as the Liberty Tree. A label on the breast of Oliver's effigy praised liberty and

denounced "Vengeance on the Subverters of it," and another label warned: "He that takes this down is an enemy to his country." At sunset, forty or fifty artisans and tradesmen took down the effigies and carried them in a procession to Andrew Oliver's dock, where the mob leveled a building they believed would be the stamp office. The procession was followed by a great concourse of people, some of the highest reputation and in the greatest order. At this point, the less genteel members of the mob proceeded to wreak havoc on Andrew Oliver's house, pulling down fences, breaking windows, looking glasses, and furniture, stripping his trees of fruit, and drinking his wine. *SCRIBE* Three days later, Andrew Oliver resigned his commission as Stamp Master.

12 *JOHN DICKINSON* With an unexampled unanimity, the people compelled the stamp officers throughout the provinces to resign their employments. The virtuous indignation with which they acted was inspired by their generous love of liberty. For the resignation of the officers was judged the most effectual and the most decent method of preventing the execution of a statute that strikes the axe into the root of the tree and lays the hitherto flourishing branches of American freedom, with all its precious fruits, low in the dust.

SCRIBE Ten months after it was authorized by the British Parliament, the Stamp Act was repealed. But rather than ending British tyranny, the colonists quickly learned that the tyranny had just begun.

13 *SAMUEL ADAMS* Whereas it appears by an act of the British Parliament passed in the last sessions, that the East India Company is by the said act allowed to export their teas into America, in such quantities as the Lord of the Treasury shall judge proper; and that the tribute of three pence on every pound of tea is to be enacted by the detestable task masters there. Upon the due consideration thereof:

Resolved, that the disposal of their own property is the inherent right of freemen; that there can be no property in that which another can of right take from us without our consent; that the claim of Parliament to tax America is in other words a claim of right to buy contributions on us at pleasure;

Second, that the duty imposed by Parliament upon tea landed in America is a tax on the Americans without their consent;

Third, that the express purpose for which the tax is levied on the Americans, namely for the support of government and the defense of His Majesty's dominions in America, has a direct tendency to introduce arbitrary government and slavery;

Fourth, that a virtuous and steady opposition to the ministerial plan of governing America is a duty which every freeman in America owes to his country, to himself, and to his posterity;

Fifth, that the resolutions lately come by the East India Company to send out their teas to America is an open attempt to enforce the ministerial plan and a violent attack upon the liberties of America;

Sixth, that it is the duty of every American to oppose this attempt;

Seventh, that whoever shall directly or indirectly countenance this attempt—or in any wise aid or abet in unloading, receiving, or vending the tea is an enemy to America!

SCRIBE On the sixteenth of December, 1773, as three ships loaded with tea sat in the Boston Harbor, seven thousand angry colonists gathered at the Old South Meeting House in Boston, both Loyalists and Patriots:

14 *PATRIOT JOSIAH QUINCY* It is not, Mr. Moderator, the spirit that vapors within these walls that must stand us in stead. The exertions of

this day will call forth events which will make a very different spirit necessary for our salvation. Whoever supposes that shouts and hosannas will terminate the trials of the day entertains a childish fancy!

15 *LOYALIST HARRISON GRAY* Sir, this is a most dangerous proceeding. You risk, Sir, prosecution for treason for your intemperate language!

16 *JOSIAH QUINCY* If the old gentleman in the gallery intends by his warning to the young man on the floor to utter only a friendly voice in the spirit of paternal advice, I thank him. If his object be to terrify and intimidate, I despise him. Personally, perhaps, I have less concern than anyone present in the crisis which is approaching. Yet the seeds of dissolution, Sir, are thickly planted in my constitution, and they must soon ripen!

17 *JOSIAH QUINCY* My friends, we must be grossly ignorant of the importance and value of the prize for which we contend. We must be equally ignorant of the power of those who have combined against us. We must be blind to that malice, inveteracy, and insatiable revenge which actuate our enemies, public and private, abroad and in our bosom, to hope that we shall end this controversy without the sharpest conflicts; and to flatter ourselves that popular pleas, popular harangues, popular acclamations, and popular vapor will vanquish our foes. Let us consider the issue. Let us look to the end. Let us weigh and consider those measures which must bring on the most trying and terrible result this country ever saw! 18 *JOSIAH QUINCY* For I see the clouds which now rise thick and fast upon our horizon, the thunder rolls, and the lightnings play, and to that God who rides on the whirlwind and directs the storm, I commit my country!

19 *SAMUEL ADAMS* As the meeting continued, the people were resolved

that the tea should not be landed but sent back to London in the same bottom. The owner of the vessel, Mr. Rotch, acquainted them that the governor had refused to grant him a passport to return the tea to England, thinking it inconsistent with the laws and his duty to the king. [20 SAMUEL ADAMS] At that moment we knew the meeting could do nothing more to save the country.

[21 SAMUEL ADAMS] The people, finding all their endeavors for this purpose thus totally frustrated, dissolved the meeting which had consisted by common estimation of at least seven thousand men, many of whom had come from towns at the distance of twenty miles. [22 JOHN ANDREWS] There was a confused murmur among the members as the meeting dissolved, many of them crying out, "Let every man do his duty and be true to his country"; and there was a general huzzah for Griffin's Wharf.

[23 JOHN ANDREWS] It was now evening, and I immediately dressed myself in the costume of an Indian, equipped with a small hatchet which I and my associates denominated the tomahawk, with which and a club—after having painted my face and hands with coal dust in the shop of a blacksmith—I repaired to Griffin's Wharf, where the ships lay that contained the tea. When I first appeared in the street after being thus disguised, I fell in with many who were dressed, equipped, and painted as I was and who fell in with me and marched in order to the place of our destination. When we arrived at the wharf, there were three of our number who assumed an authority to direct our operations, to which we readily submitted.

They divided us into three parties, for the purpose of boarding the three ships which contained the tea at the same time. We were immediately ordered by the respective commanders to board all the ships at the same time, which we promptly obeyed.

The commander of the division to which I belonged, as soon as we were on board the ship, appointed me boatswain, and ordered me to go to the captain and demand of him the keys to the hatches and a dozen candles. I made the demand accordingly, and the captain promptly replied, and delivered the articles, but requested me at the same time to do no damage to the ship or rigging. We then were ordered by our commander to open the hatches and take out all the chests of tea and throw them overboard, and we immediately proceeded to execute his orders, first cutting and splitting the chests with our tomahawks, so as thoroughly to expose them to the effects of the water.

In about three hours from the time we went on board, we had thus broken and thrown overboard every tea chest to be found in the ship, while those in the other ships were disposing of the tea in the same way at the same time.

We then quietly retired to our several places of residence, without having any conversation with each other, or taking any measures to discover who were our associates; nor do I recollect of our having had the knowledge of the name of a single individual concerned in that affair. There appeared to be an understanding that each individual should volunteer his services, keep his own secret, and risk the consequence for himself.

[24] *SAMUEL ADAMS* In less than four hours every chest of tea on board three ships which had by this time arrived, three hundred and forty-two chests, or rather the contents of them, was thrown into the sea without the least injury to the vessels or any other property.

[25] *JOHN ADAMS* This is the most magnificent movement of all. There is a dignity, a majesty, a sublimity, in this last effort of the patriots that I greatly admire. The people should never rise, without

doing something to be remembered, something notable and striking. This destruction of the tea is so bold, so daring, so firm, so intrepid and inflexible, and it must have so important consequences and so lasting that I can't but consider it as an epoch in history. 26 *JOHN ADAMS* My friends, the die is cast. The people have passed the river and cut away the bridge.

27 *ALEXANDER HAMILTON* When the first principles of civil society are violated, and the rights of a whole people are invaded, the common forms of municipal law are not to be regarded. Men may then betake themselves to the law of nature; and if they but conform their actions to that standard, all cavils† against them betray either ignorance or dishonesty. For there are some events in society to which human laws can not extend; but when applied to them, lose all their force and efficacy. In short, when human laws contradict or discountenance the means which are necessary to preserve the essential rights of any society, they defeat the proper ends of all laws, and so become null and void.

SCRIBE The British reacted to the Boston Tea Party by punishing all the people of New England. The Boston Port Act closed the port of Boston, cutting off the people from all shipments, including food and garment, until the colonists paid for the tea. Likewise, The Massachusetts Government Act reduced the power of the Massachusetts legislature and increased the power of the royal governor. The Administration of Justice Act allowed British officials accused of crimes to be tried in England instead of in the colonies. The Quartering Act required colonists to provide housing and supplies for British troops.

28 *SAMUEL ADAMS* For flagrant injustice and barbarity, one might

---

† Cavils: petty objections.

search in vain among the archives of Constantinople to find a match for the Boston Port Act. But what else could have been expected from a parliament too long under the dictates and control of an administration which seems to be totally lost to all sense and feeling of morality, and governed by passion, cruelty, and revenge? For us to reason against such an act would be idleness. Our business is to find means to evade its malignant design. The inhabitants view it not with astonishment, but with indignation. They discover the utmost contempt of the framers of it.

29 *SONS OF LIBERTY NOTICE* To pass through the fire at six o'clock this evening, in honor to the immortal goddess of liberty, the late infamous act of the British Parliament for further distressing the American colonies; the place of execution will be the public parade where all Sons of Liberty are desired to attend.

30 *LOCAL NEWSPAPER* Accordingly, a very numerous and respectable body were assembled of near one thousand people when a huge pole, forty-five feet high, was erected and consecrated to the shrine of liberty, after which the act of Parliament for blocking up the Boston Harbor was read aloud, sentenced to the flames, and executed by the hands of the common hangman. Then the following resolutions were read.

Be it resolved:

That it is the greatest dignity, interest, and happiness of every American that our liberties are duly secured;

That the present ministry, being instigated by the devil and led on by their wicked and corrupt hearts, have a design to take away our liberties and properties and to enslave us forever;

That the late act which their malice hath caused to be passed in

Parliament, for blocking up the port of Boston, is unjust, illegal, and oppressive;

That those pimps and parasites who dared to advise their master to such detestable measures be held in utter abhorrence by us and every American and their names loaded with the curses of all succeeding generations;

That we scorn the chains of slavery and despise every attempt to rivet them upon us;

That we are the sons of freedom and resolved that, till time shall be no more, God-like virtue shall blazon our hemisphere!

31 *SONS OF LIBERTY SONG*

> With the beasts of the wood, we will ramble for food,
> And lodge in wild deserts and caves.
>
> And live as poor as Job, on the skirts of the globe,
> Before we submit to be Slaves.
>
> The birthright we hold, shall never be sold,
> But sacred maintained to our graves.
>
> Nay, and 'ere we'll comply, we will gallantly die,
> For we must not and will not be slaves!
>
> Brave boys, we must not, and will not be slaves!

Chapter Seven
United

[1] *SAMUEL ADAMS* This town has received the copy of the Boston Port Act of the British Parliament, wherein it appears that we have been tried and condemned, and are to be punished by the shutting up of the harbor and other marks of revenge until we shall disgrace ourselves by servilely yielding up, in effect, the just and righteous claims of America.

If the parliament had a right to pass such an edict, does it not discover the want of every moral principle to proceed to the destruction of a community, without even the accusation of any crime committed by such community? There is no crime alleged, as committed by the town of Boston, in the act. Outrages have been committed within the town, and therefore the community, as such, are to be destroyed?

[2] *SAMUEL ADAMS* Thus in order to ascertain the sense of the people, a committee is now appointed—of which our patriot Otis is chairman—to open a free communication with the towns of this province and colonies of British America. [3] *SAMUEL ADAMS* We will prepare a statement of the rights of the colonists and of this province in particular, as men, as Christians, and as subjects—a letter to be sent to every colony and to the world, giving the sense of this town. [4] *SAMUEL ADAMS* The soon this is done, I think the

better. I have received letters from Marblehead and Newburyport fraught with manly resentment. Whenever the friends of the country shall be assured of each others' sentiments, that spirit which is necessary will not be wanting.

5 *BOSTON COMMITTEE OF CORRESPONDENCE,* May 12, 1774: Gentlemen, the evils which we have long foreseen are now come upon this town and province—the long meditated stroke is now given to the civil liberty of this country. The bill for blocking up the harbor of Boston is replete with injustice and cruelty. Thousands of innocent men, besides women and infants, are by it reduced to indigence and distress.

We trust in God that our countrymen never will submit to these shameful impositions. For if any should think that this town alone is to groan under the weight of arbitrary power, we are now furnished by our enemies with a still more glaring evidence of a fixed plan of the British administration to bring the whole continent into the most humiliating bondage. For though we in this town more immediately feel this distress, yet our brethren in the other towns of this province, and all the other colonies, must see that we suffer in the common cause, and that they themselves must soon realize the sufferings under which we now labor, if no means are discovered for our relief.

6 *ALEXANDER HAMILTON* If the rest of America passively looks on while a sister colony is subjugated, the same fate will gradually overtake all. The safety of the whole depends upon the mutual protection of every part. If the sword of oppression be permitted to lop off one limb without opposition, reiterated strokes will soon dismember the whole body. Hence it is the duty and interest of all the colonies to succor and support the one which is suffering. It is sometimes sagaciously urged that we ought to commiserate

the distresses of the people of Massachusetts, but not intermeddle in their affairs so far as perhaps to bring ourselves into like circumstances with them. This might be good reasoning, if our neutrality would not be more dangerous than our participation. But I am unable to conceive how the colonies in general would have any security against oppression if they were once to content themselves with barely pitying each other, while Parliament was prosecuting and enforcing its demands. Unless they continually protect and assist each other, they must all inevitably fall prey to their enemies.

SCRIBE The people united in support of Boston as shipments of supplies and food poured in from across the colonies.

7 BALTIMORE COMMITTEE OF CORRESPONDENCE Gentlemen, by order of the Committee of Correspondence for this town, we have shipped on board the sloop *America*—Perkins Allen, Master—three thousand bushels of corn, twenty barrels of rye flour, two barrels of pork, and twenty barrels of bread, for the relief of our brethren, the distressed inhabitants of your town. The good people of this province, who have in general discovered a hearty disposition to sympathy in your grievances, will generously contribute to maintain and support every sufferer in your and their common cause.

8 KINGSTON, NEW HAMPSHIRE COMMITTEE OF CORRESPONDENCE Gentlemen, the inhabitants of Kingston, in the province of New Hampshire, see with deep concern the unhappy misunderstanding and disagreement that now subsists between Great Britain and these American colonies.

We look on the cause in which you are engaged as a common cause, and we and our posterity are equally interested with you in the event. This town has contributed and sent by the bearers hereof one hundred sheep as a present for their relief to be disposed of as you see fit.

9 *ESSEX COUNTY, VIRGINIA COMMITTEE OF CORRESPONDENCE* Gentlemen, this serves to inform you that we have consigned to you, by the schooner *Sally*—James Perkins, Master—one thousand and eighty-seven bushels of Indian corn, for the use of our suffering brethren in your town. The remainder, amounting to four or five hundred bushels, shall come by the first opportunity. We can venture to assure you that the Virginians are warmly disposed to assist you and hope for your steady and prudent perseverance in the common cause of our country. We pray God for a happy relief to our virtuous struggles, and we beg leave to assure you that we have the most sincere regard for our northward brethren, and are your most obedient servants.

10 *DURHAM, NEW HAMPSHIRE COMMITTEE OF CORRESPONDENCE* Gentlemen, we take pleasure in transmitting to you by Mr. Scammel, a few cattle with a small sum of money, which a number of persons in this place, tenderly sympathizing with our suffering brethren in Boston, have contributed towards their support. With this or soon after, you will receive the donations of a number in Lee, a parish lately set off from this town, and in a few days those of Dover, Newmarket, and other adjacent towns. What you herewith receive comes not from the opulent, but mostly from the industrious yeomanry in this parish. We have but a few persons of affluent fortunes among us, but those have most cheerfully contributed to the relief of the distressed in your metropolis.

This is considered by us, not as a gift or an act of charity, but of justice—as a small part of what we are in duty bound to communicate to those truly noble and patriotic advocates of American freedom who are bravely standing in the gap between us and slavery, defending the common interests of a whole continent and gloriously struggling in the cause of liberty. Upon you the eyes of all America are fixed. Upon your invincible patience, fortitude, and resolution under God depends all that is dear to them and their prosperity.

May that superintendent gracious Being, whose ears are ever open to the cry of the oppressed, turn the counsels of our enemies into foolishness, deliver us from the hands of our oppressors, and make those very measures by which they are endeavoring to compass our destruction, the means of fixing our invaluable rights and privileges upon a more firm and lasting basis.

11 *BROOKLYN, IN POMFRET, CONNECTICUT COMMITTEE OF CORRESPONDENCE* Gentlemen, with our hearts deeply impressed with the feelings of humanity towards our near and dear brethren of Boston who are now suffering under a ministerial, revengeful hand; and at the same time full of gratitude to the patriotic inhabitants for the noble stand which they have made against all oppressive innovations, we send you one hundred and twenty-five sheep as a present from the inhabitants of the parish of Brooklyn, hoping thereby you may be enabled to stand more firm, if possible, in the glorious cause in which you are embarked. In zeal in our country's cause, we are exceeded by none; but our abilities and opportunities do not admit of our being of that weight in the American scale as we would to God we were.

We mean, in the first place, to attempt to appease the fire (raised by your committing the India tea to the watery element as a merited oblation to Neptune) of an ambitious and vindictive minister, by the blood of rams and of lambs. If that does not answer the end, we are ready to march in the van and to sprinkle the American altars with our hearts blood, if occasion should be.

Here we have an unbounded, fertile country worth contending for with blood. Here bribery and corruption, which are certain forebodings of a speedy dissolution, are as yet only known by names. The public virtue now exhibited by the Americans exceeds all of its kind that can be produced in the annals of the Greeks and Romans. Behold them from north to south, from east to west, striving to comfort the town of Boston, both by publishing their sentiments in regard to the present tyrannical administration, and by supporting their poor with provision. You are held up as a spectacle to the whole world. All Christendom are longing to see the event of the American contest!

12 *VIRGINIA LEGISLATURE* We are clearly of opinion that an attack made on one of our sister colonies, to compel submission to arbitrary taxes, is an attack made on all British America and threatens ruin to the rights of all, unless the united wisdom of the whole be applied. And for this purpose it is recommended to the Committee of Correspondence, that they communicate, with their several corresponding committees, on the expediency of appointing deputies from the several colonies of British America, to meet in general Congress at such place annually as shall be thought most convenient; there to deliberate on those general measures which the united interests of America may from time to time require.

SCRIBE The First Continental Congress of the colonies met in Philadelphia on September 5, 1774.

13 *BOSTON PROPOSAL* Gentlemen, there is but one way that we can conceive of to prevent what is to be deprecated by all good men, and ought by all possible means to be prevented—namely, the horrors that must follow an open rupture between Great Britain and her colonies, or on our part, a subjection to absolute slavery: By affecting the trade and interest of Great Britain so deeply as

shall induce her to withdraw her oppressive hand. There can be no doubt of our succeeding to the utmost of our wishes if we universally come into a solemn league not to import goods from Great Britain and not to buy any goods that shall hereafter be imported from thence until our grievances shall be redressed. To these, or even to the least of these shameful impositions, we trust in God, our countrymen never will submit. [14] *JOSIAH QUINCY* For Americans have one common interest to unite them. That interest must cement them. Natural allies, the colonies have published to the world professions of reciprocal esteem and confidence, aid and assistance; they have pledged their faith of mutual friendship and alliance. Not only common danger, bondage, and disgrace, but national truth and honor conspire to make the colonists resolve—TO STAND OR FALL TOGETHER!

[15] *RESOLVES OF THE FIRST CONTINENTAL CONGRESS* Resolved, that from and after the first day of December, we will not import into British America, from Great Britain or Ireland, any goods, wares, or merchandise whatsoever, or from any other place any such goods, wares, or merchandise, as shall have been exported from Great Britain or Ireland; nor will we, after that day, import any East India tea from any part of the world, nor any molosses, syrups, paneles,† coffee, or pimenta from the British plantations, or from Dominica, nor wines from Madeira or the Western Islands, nor foreign indigo.

Resolved, that the Committee of Correspondence, in the respective colonies do frequently inspect the entries of their customs houses and inform each other from time to time of the true state thereof and of every other material circumstance that may occur relative to this association.

---

† Paneles: unrefined cane sugar.

Resolved, that all manufactures of this country be sold at reasonable prices, so that no undue advantage be taken of a future scarcity of goods.

Resolved, that we do further agree and resolve that we will have no trade, commerce, dealings, or intercourse whatsoever with any colony or province in North America, which shall not accede to, or which shall hereafter violate, this association, but will hold them as unworthy of the rights of freemen and as inimical to the liberties of their country.

Resolved, that a committee be chosen in every county, city, and town by those who are qualified to vote for representatives in the legislature, whose business it shall be attentively to observe the conduct of all persons touching this association; and when it shall be made to appear, to the satisfaction of a majority of any such committee that any person within the limits of their appointment has violated this association, that such majority do forthwith cause the truth of the case to be published in the gazette, to the end that all such foes to the rights of British America may be publicly known and universally condemned as the enemies of American liberty; and thence forth, we respectively will break off all dealings with him or her.

SCRIBE The colonies united in support of the boycott. [16] *ALBEMARLE COUNTY, VIRGINIA COMMITTEE OF CORRESPONDENCE* It is the opinion of this meeting that we immediately cease to import all commodities from every part of the world which are subjected by the British Parliament; that it is the opinion of this meeting that these measures should be pursued until a repeal be obtained of the act for blocking up the harbor of Boston; of the acts prohibiting or restraining internal manufactures in America; of the acts imposing on any commodities duties to be paid in America; and of the acts laying restrictions on the American trade!

17 *NEW YORK PATRIOTS* We have thus sent committees to the several contractors to let them know if they supplied any further, they would incur the resentment of the whole country; and at the same time signified to our Committee of Correspondence that we agree that the workmen here are no longer eligible to go on preparing houses, as we might possibly by persisting, not only incur blame from our sister colonies, but essentially affect the union now subsisting between town and country.

18 *NEWBURYPORT, MASSACHUSETTS COMMITTEE OF CORRESPONDENCE* The merchants of Newburyport will not trade to the southward of South Carolina, nor to any part of Great Britain and Ireland, till the harbor of Boston is again open and free; or till the disputes between Britain and the colonies are settled. 19 *WORCESTER, MASSACHUESETTS* The yeomanry of our country towns have thus signed a covenant not to purchase any British manufactures imported from that island!

20 *JOHN ADAMS* My friends, the complete accomplishment of the Committees of Correspondence in so short a time, and by such simple means, was perhaps a singular example in the history of mankind. Thirteen clocks were made to strike together as one: a perfection of mechanism, which no artist had ever before effected.

21 *DAVID RAMSAY* In the counties and towns of the several provinces, as well as in the cities, the people assembled and passed resolutions expressive of their rights and of their detestation of the late American acts of Parliament. These had an instantaneous effect on the minds of thousands. Not only the young and impetuous, but the aged and temperate, joined in pronouncing them to be unconstitutional and oppressive. They viewed them as deadly weapons aimed at the vitals of that liberty which they adored, as rendering

abortive the generous pains taken by their forefathers to procure for them in a new world the quiet enjoyment of their rights. A patriotic flame, created and diffused by the contagion of sympathy, was communicated to so many breasts and reflected from such a variety of objects, as to become too intense to be resisted. This season of universal distress exhibited a striking proof of how practicable it is for mankind to sacrifice ease, pleasure, and interest, when the mind is strongly excited by its passions. In the midst of their sufferings, cheerfulness appeared in the face of all the people. They counted everything cheap in comparison with liberty and readily gave up whatever tended to endanger it. A noble strain of generosity and mutual support was generally excited. A great and powerful diffusion of public spirit took place. The animation of the times raised the actors in these scenes above themselves and excited them to deeds of self-denial which the interested prudence of calmer seasons can scarcely credit.

22 *HANNAH WINTHROP* Let it be known unto Britain, that American daughters are politicians and patriots! 23 *ESTHER REED* The time is arrived when we shall display the same sentiments which animated us when we renounced the use of teas rather than receive them from our persecutors. We will place former necessaries in the rank of superfluities, and our republican and laborious hands will spin the flax and prepare the linen! For should we hesitate to wear a clothing more simple; hair dressed less elegant, while at the price of this small privation, we would deserve your benedictions. Who, amongst us, will not renounce with the highest pleasure, those vain ornaments, when she shall consider that the valiant defenders of America will be able to draw some advantage from the money which she may have laid out in these? That our brave men will be better defended from the rigors of the seasons? That these presents will perhaps be valued by them

at a greater price when they will have it in their power to say, "This is the offering of the ladies!"? [24] *SAMUEL ADAMS* And with the ladies on our side, we will make every Tory tremble!

[25] *SARAH FULTON* The Daughters of Liberty, young ladies of good reputation, assembled at the house of Doctor Ephraim Bowen. There they exhibited a fine example of industry by spinning from sunrise until dark, and displayed a spirit for saving their sinking country rarely to be found among persons of more age and experience. [26] *VIRGINIA GAZETTE* Thus have all assemblies of American ladies exhibited a like example of public virtue and private economy, as they have united in making homespun dress. [27] *LOCAL NEWSPAPER* In truth, I presume there never was a time when, or a place where, the spinning wheel could more influence the affairs of men, than at present in this and the neighboring colonies.

[28] *ANONYMOUS*

> Young ladies in town, and those that live round,
> wear none but your own country linen.
> Of economy boast, let your pride be the most,
> to show clothes of your own make and spinnin'.
> "What if homespun," they say, "be not quite as gay,
> as brocades?" Be not in a passion.
> For once it is known, 'tis much worn in town,
> one and all will cry out, "'Tis the fashion!".
> And as one all agree, that you'll not married be,
> to such as will wear London factory.
> But at first sight refuse, tell 'em you will choose,
> as encourage our own manufactory.
> No more ribbons wear, nor in rich silks appear,
> love your country much better than fine things.
> Begin without passion, 'twill soon be the fashion,

to grace your smooth locks with a twine string.
Throw away your bohea,† and your green hyson tea,
and all things of a new fashioned duty.
Get in a good store, of the choice Labrador,
there'll soon be enough here to suit ye.
These do without fear, and to all you'll appear,
Fair, charming, true, lovely, and clever,
Though the times remain darkish,
young men will be sparkish,
and love you much stronger than ever.

29 *ELIZABETH ADKINS* When the exactions of the Mother Country had rendered it impossible for any but the wealthiest to import anything to eat or wear, and all had to be raised and manufactured at home—from bread stuffs, sugar, and rum to the linen and woolen for our clothes and bedding—you may well imagine that my duties were not light, though I can say for myself that I never complained, even in my inmost thoughts. 30 *TEMPERANCE SMITH* To tell the truth, I had no leisure for murmuring. I rose with the sun and all through the long day, I had no time for aught but my work. So much did it press upon me that I could scarcely divert my thoughts from its demands, even during the family prayers, which thing both amazed and displeased me, for during that hour, at least, I should have been sending all my thoughts to heaven for the safety of my beloved husband and the salvation of our hapless country. Instead of which, I was often wondering whether Polly had remembered to set the sponge for the bread, or to put water on the leach tub, or to turn the cloth in the dying vat, or whether wool had been carded for Betsey to start her spinning wheel in the morning, or Billy had chopped light wood

---

†   Bohea: a black Chinese tea.

enough for the kindling, or dry hard wood enough to heat the big oven, or whether some other thing had not been forgotten of the thousand that must be done without fail, or else there would be a disagreeable hitch in the housekeeping.

SCRIBE The boycott achieved great effect. Imported goods from Great Britain fell by half over the previous year, from 420,000 to 208,000 pounds. But the tyrannical Acts of the King and Parliament remained.

SCRIBE Meanwhile, tensions grew and a rumor spread throughout the New England countryside that British Regulars had not only seized some powder but also killed six patriots and set Boston ablaze. The news ran rampant, and in no time some 40,000 men from every village and hamlet for hundreds of miles headed toward Boston to confront the Redcoats. From Worchester County alone, 6,000 took to the road, bearing what arms they could. A traveler from Connecticut reported, "They scarcely left half a dozen men in a town, unless old and decrepit, and in one town the landlord told him that himself was the only man left." An observer described the frenzy of the moment:

"All along were armed men rushing forward, some on foot, some on horseback; at every house women and children making cartridges, running bullets, making wallets, baking biscuits, crying and bemoaning, and at the same time animating their husbands and sons to fight for their liberties, though not knowing whether they should ever see them again. But alas, it was a false alarm. 'The people seemed really disappointed,' one man told John Adams two months later, when the news was contradicted."

SCRIBE As war drew near boys and men from across the colonies joined their local militia.

31 *MINUTEMEN COVENANT* We whose names are hereunto subscribed, do voluntarily enlist ourselves as Minutemen, to be ready for military operation upon the shortest notice. We hereby promise and engage that we will immediately, each of us, provide for and equip himself with an effective firearm, bayonet, pouch, knapsack, and thirty rounds of cartridges ready made; and that we may obtain the skill of complete soldiers, we promise to convene for exercise in the art military at least twice every week, and oftener if our officers shall think necessary.

SON Father, with the obstinacy of the British, fighting becomes today open. I would gladly expose myself, or hold my life more cheap.

FATHER Son, your spirited declarations of readiness to bleed in your country's cause may sound well enough late at night at the tavern. I entertain no doubt of your bravery and firmness; yet my dear son, I should be extremely deficient in my duty if I forbore to tell you freely, that talking and writing of the "cheapness" of one's life bears no mark of either. Reserve your life for your country's call, but wait the call.

SCRIBE The call soon came.

32 *JOHN HANCOCK* To the brave men of the militia, their delegates in Congress now make the most solemn appeal: They are called upon to say whether they will live slaves or die freemen. They are requested to step forth in defense of their wives, their children, their liberty, and every thing they hold dear. The Cause is certainly a most glorious one; and I hope every man in these colonies is determined to see it gloriously ended, or to perish in the ruins of it!

SCRIBE Five hundred militias comprised of 230,000 patriot soldiers from across the colonies answered the call to fight for their liberty.

33 *JOSIAH QUINCY* Patriots, when I reflect on the exalted character of our forefathers, on the fortitude of our illustrious predecessors, on the noble struggles of the late memorable period – and from these reflections, when I contemplate the gloomy aspect of the present day, my heart is alternately torn with doubt and hope, despondency and terror. Can the true, generous magnanimity of our heroes be entirely lost in their degenerate progeny? Is the genius of liberty, which so late inflamed our bosoms, fled forever?

34 *DANIEL WEBSTER* It is simple to follow the easy and familiar path of personal ambition and private gain. It is more comfortable to sit content in the easy approval of friends and of neighbors than to risk the friction and the controversy that comes with public affairs. It is easier to fall in step with the slogans of others than to march to the beat of the internal drummer – to make and stand on judgements of your own.

35 *JOSIAH QUINCY* Your enemies pretend to be sanguine that your avarice of commercial riches has dissolved your union and mutual confidence; that your boasted courage is but vapor; and that your perseverance will be as the morning cloud.

SCRIBE Sadly, my fellow patriots, we must acknowledge some melancholy truth in this sentiment. 36 *JOHN ADAMS* For the true source of our sufferings has been our timidity. 37 *BENJAMIN FRANKLIN* And as we must account for every idle word, so must we account for every idle silence.

38 *JOSIAH QUINCY* Yet there is not a sensible man in both parties but acknowledges your ability to save your country if you have but union, courage, and perseverance. 39 *JOSIAH QUINCY* Will a temporary advantage seduce you from your duty? Will you not evidence at this time, how much you despise a commercial bribe and testify

to the world that you do not vail to the most glorious of the ancients, in love of freedom and sternness of virtue?

40 JOSIAH QUINCY Be not deceived, my countrymen. Believe not those venal hirelings when they would cajole you by their subtleties into submission or frighten you by their vaporings into compliance. When they strive to flatter you by the terms 'moderation and prudence,' tell them, that calmness and deliberation are to guide the judgment; courage and intrepidity command the action. When they endeavor to make us 'perceive our inability to oppose such a great force', let us boldly answer: In defense of our civil and religious rights, we dare oppose the world; blandishments† will not fascinate us, nor will threats of a 'halter'‡ intimidate. For under God, we are determined, that wheresoever, whensoever, or howsoever, we shall be called to make our exit, we will die freemen!!!

41 JOHN HANCOCK Sons of liberty, resistance to tyranny is the Christian and social duty of each individual! *42 SAMUEL WEST* It is an indispensable duty, which we owe to God and our country, to rouse up and bestir ourselves – to be animated with a noble zeal for the sacred cause of liberty!

43 DANIEL WEBSTER This duty pursues us ever. If we take to ourselves the wings of the morning, and dwell in the uttermost parts of the sea, this duty performed or violated is still with us. If we say the darkness shall cover us, in the darkness as in the light this duty is yet with us. *44 W.E. CHANNING* We must have contempt of all outward things which come in competition with this duty. We must have a readiness to sacrifice life's highest material good, and life itself. For it is confirmed by all experience, it is sanctioned by

---

†   A flattering statement used to persuade.
‡   The noose used by a hangman.

conscience, and it is the chief dictate of the universal and eternal lawgiver, that everything must be yielded up for the right!

45 *DANIEL WEBSTER* Patriots! Nothing will ruin the country if the people themselves will unite to undertake its safety! And nothing can save it, if they leave that safety in any hands but their own! 46 *SAMUEL ADAMS* For it does not take a majority to prevail, but rather an irate, tireless minority, keen on setting brushfires of freedom in the minds of men!!!

47 *NATHANIEL NILES* And if any should say that it is in vain for them as individuals to be vigilant, zealous, and firm in pursuing any measures for the security of our rights, unless all would unite, I would reply: Ages are composed of seconds, the earth of sands, and the sea of drops too small to be seen by the naked eye. The smallest particles have their influence. Such is our state, that each individual has a proportion of influence on some neighbor at least; he, on another, and so on. As in a river, the following drop urges that which is before, and every one through the whole length of the stream has the like influence. We know not what individuals may do. We are not at liberty to lie dormant until we can, at once, influence the whole. We must begin with the weight we have. Should the little springs neglect to flow until a general agreement should take place, the torrent that now bears down all before it would never be formed. These mighty floods have their rise in single drops from the rocks, which, upon uniting, creep along until they meet with another combination so small that it might be absorbed by creeks and streams. These then unite, proceed, and enlarge until mountains tremble at their sound. Let us receive instruction from the streams, and, without discouragement, pursue a laudable plan. 48 *THOMAS PAINE* For it is not in numbers, but in unity, that our great strength lies.

Chapter Eight
Declaration

[1] *JOSEPH WARREN* When I behold my country, once the seat of industry, peace, and plenty, changed by Englishmen to a theater of blood and misery, Heaven forgive me if I cannot root out those passions which it has implanted in my bosom and detest submission to a people who have either ceased to be human, or have not virtue enough to feel their own wretchedness and servitude.

Recollect who are the men that demand your submission, to whose decrees you are invited to pay obedience! Men who—unmindful of their relation to you as brethren; of your long, implicit submission to their laws; and of the sacrifice which you and your forefathers made—formed a deliberate plan to wrest from you the small pittance of property which they had permitted you to acquire. Remember that the men who wish to rule over you are they who, in pursuit of this plan of despotism, annulled the sacred contracts which had been made with your ancestors; men who called your patience, cowardice; your piety, hypocrisy.

[2] *GEORGE WASHINGTON* Satisfied as I am that the British Parliament are trampling upon the valuable rights of Americans, confirmed to them by charter and constitution they themselves boast of, and convinced beyond the smallest doubt, that these measures are the result of deliberation, and attempted to be carried into

execution by the hand of power, is it a time to trifle, or risk our cause upon petitions? Or should we go on to bear more, and forbear to enumerate our just causes of complaint?

SCRIBE Through the Intolerable Acts, the king and Parliament starved and jailed colonists, plundering both their wealth and rights. Outrage soon boiled over into the bloody battles of Lexington and Concord, setting the stage for the Second Continental Congress. As the colonies prepared for war, each town and district sent a delegate to the Philadelphia congress and provided their representatives with written instructions as to their limitations and duties.

3 *NATICK TOWNSHIP, MASSACHUSETTS* In a meeting of the town of Natick, in consequence of a resolve being laid before the town, setting forth the obligations that lie upon every town in this colony 4 *BUCKINGHAM COUNTY, VIRGINIA* you were elected and deputed by us to fill the most difficult and important places that the representatives of this county were ever appointed to act in; we cannot help but, in justice to ourselves and posterity, forbear to give some instructions concerning the discharge of your great trust.

5 *CHERAWS DISTRICT, SOUTH CAROLINA* When a people—born and bred in a land of freedom and virtue; uncorrupted by those refinements which effeminate and debase the mind; manly and generous in their sentiments; bold and hardy in their nature; and actuated by every principle of liberality—from experience are convinced of the wicked schemes of their treacherous rulers to fetter them with the chains of servitude and rob them of every noble and desirable privilege which distinguishes them as freemen, justice, humanity, and the immutable laws of God justify and support them in revoking those sacred trusts which are so impiously violated.

Declaration

₆ *BUCKINGHAM COUNTY, VIRGINIA* The British Parliament has violated the faith of charters, the principles of the British Constitution, and attempted to destroy our legal as well as natural rights. They have broken through positive laws, and the ties which unite man to man in general affection, by which means they have become felons and enemies.

₇ *CHARLES COUNTY, MARYLAND* This is the cruelty and injustice of the British government, under which we have too long borne oppression and wrongs; our towns plundered, burnt, and destroyed; our friends and countrymen confined in dungeons when captivated and, as if criminals, chained down to the earth; our estates confiscated; our men, women, and children robbed and murdered!

₈ *BUCKINGHAM COUNTY, VIRGINIA* Our flourishing towns have been burnt down and demolished, ₉ *CHERAWS DISTRICT, SOUTH CAROLINA* as tyranny, violence, and injustice take the place of equity, mildness, and affection. ₁₀ *CHERAWS DISTRICT, SOUTH CAROLINA* Cast off, persecuted, defamed, given up as prey, a righteous and much injured people have at length appealed to God.

₁₁ *CHARLES COUNTY, MARYLAND* We declare, for these reasons, that our affection for the people, and allegiance to the Crown of Great Britain, so readily and truly acknowledged till of late, is forfeited; ₁₂ *NATICK TOWNSHIP, MASSACHUSETTS* that should the honorable Continental Congress declare these American colonies independent of the Kingdom of Great Britain, we will, with our lives and fortunes, join with the other inhabitants of this colony, and with those of the other colonies; ₁₃ *BUCKINGHAM COUNTY, VIRGINIA* that the people of Buckingham County will repel force by force; and, for the effectual purpose thereof, take into our own hands the legislative, executive, and judicial powers of government; ₁₄ *HALIFAX, NORTH CAROLINA* that the delegates for Halifax, North Carolina, in the Continental

Congress, are empowered to concur with the delegates of the other colonies in declaring independency!

[15] *TOPSFIELD, MASSACHUSETTS* We would not be understood that we mean to dictate, leaving that momentous affair to the well-known wisdom, prudence, justice, and integrity of that honorable body the Continental Congress. Yet having thus freely spoken our sentiments in respect to independence, we now instruct you, Sir, to give the honorable delegates of the Continental Congress the strongest assurance that if, for the safety of the United Colonies, they shall declare America to be independent of the Kingdom of Great Britain, your constituents in Topsfield will support and defend the measure with their lives and fortunes; [16] *NATICK TOWNSHIP, MASSACHUSETTS* that the people of Natick County will solemnly support with their lives and fortunes the honorable Continental Congress; [17] *ASHBY, MASSACHUSETTS* that the inhabitants of Ashby, Massachusetts, unanimously voted, will solemnly engage with their lives and fortunes to support the measure, that our latest posterity may enjoy the virtuous fruits of that work which the integrity and fortitude of the present age had, at the expense of their blood and treasure, at length happily effected.

SCRIBE As the debate raged on in the Second Continental Congress, it was Richard Henry Lee who stood to make a formal resolution for independence:

[18] *RICHARD HENRY LEE* Gentlemen, contrary to our earnest, early, and repeated petitions for peace, liberty, and safety, our enemies press us with war, threaten us with danger and slavery. [19] *RICHARD HENRY LEE* Why then, Gentlemen, why do we longer delay? Why still deliberate? Let this happy day give birth to an American republic. Let her arise, not to devastate and to conquer, but to reestablish the reign of peace and law. [20] *RICHARD HENRY LEE* Let us resolve that these

United Colonies are, and of right ought to be, free and independent states; that they are absolved from all allegiance to the British crown; and that all political connection between them and the state of Great Britain is, and ought to be, totally dissolved!

SCRIBE John Adams stood. 21 *JOHN ADAMS* I second that resolution, Sir!

22 *ELDRIDGE GERRY* In order to give the assemblies of the middle colonies an opportunity to take off their restrictions and let their delegates unite in the measure, *SCRIBE* the Second Continental Congress postponed the vote on the resolution for independence for three weeks. Several delegates from the middle colonies returned home to plead their case for an amendment to their instructions to support a resolution for independence.

23 *RESOLUTION FOR INDEPENDENCE* In the meantime, lest any time should be lost in case the Congress agrees to this resolution, we propose that a committee be appointed to prepare a Declaration to the effect of the said first resolution.

SCRIBE The Congress appointed the Committee of Five to draft a declaration of independence. The committee was comprised of:

~ Thomas Jefferson of Virginia
~ John Adams of Massachusetts
~ Benjamin Franklin of Pennsylvania
~ Roger Sherman of Connecticut
~ Robert R. Livingston of New York

24 *JOHN ADAMS* The committee met, discussed the subject, and then appointed Mr. Jefferson and me to make the draft, I suppose, because we were the two highest on the list. The sub-committee met. Jefferson proposed to me to make the draft. I said I will not.

JEFFERSON You shall do it.

ADAMS Oh, no!

JEFFERSON Why will you not? You ought to do it.

ADAMS I will not.

JEFFERSON Why?

ADAMS Reasons enough.

JEFFERSON What can be your reasons?

ADAMS Reason first: You are a Virginian, and Virginia ought to appear at the head of this business. Reason second: I am obnoxious, suspected, and unpopular; you are very much otherwise. Reason third: You can write ten times better than I can.

JEFFERSON Well, if you are decided, I will do as well as I can.

ADAMS Very well, when you have drawn it up, we will have a meeting.

25 *JOHN ADAMS* A meeting we accordingly had and conned† the paper over. I was delighted with its high tone and the flights of oratory with which it abounded, especially that concerning negro slavery, which though I knew his Southern brethren would never suffer to pass in Congress, I certainly never would oppose.

26 *JOHN ADAMS* We reported it to the Committee of Five. It was read and I do not remember that Franklin or Sherman criticized anything. We were all in haste; Congress was impatient, and the instrument was reported, as I believe, in Jefferson's handwriting as he first drew it. Congress cut off about a quarter part of it, as

---

† Conned: studied or examined closely.

I expected they would, but they obliterated some of the best of it and left all that was exceptionable. *SCRIBE* The Southern states did indeed remove Mr. Jefferson's complaint against the King for the institution of slavery in America, but most of the complaints remained.

27 *DANIEL WEBSTER* Let us, then, bring before us the assembly which was about to decide a question thus big with the fate of empire. Let us open their doors and look upon their deliberations. Let us survey the anxious and care-worn countenances; let us hear the firm-toned voices of this band of patriots.

28 *JOHN ADAMS* Mr. Dickinson conducted the debate of the declaration, not only with great ingenuity and eloquence, but with equal politeness and candor—and was answered in the same spirit.

29 *JOHN HANCOCK, MASSACHUSETTS* Gentlemen, some boast of being friends to government; I am a friend to righteous government, to a government founded upon the principles of reason and justice; but I glory in publicly avowing my eternal enmity to tyranny!

30 *WILLIAM HOOPER, NORTH CAROLINA* Truly, Gentlemen, Britain has lost us by a series of impolitic, wicked, savage actions as would disgrace a nation of uncivilized men. Human patience can bear no more, and all ranks of people cry that the cup of bitterness is running over!

31 *ABRAHAM CLARK, NEW JERSEY* At this very moment General Howe with a large armament is advancing towards New York, our Congress must resolve to declare the United Colonies free and independent states. For it is gone so far that we must now be a free independent state or a conquered country!

32 *STEPHEN HOPKINS, RHODE ISLAND* Hear! Hear! It is the power and ball

that will decide this question. The gun and the bayonet alone will furnish the contest in which we are now engaged, and any of you who cannot bring your minds to this mode of adjusting the question had better retire in time!

33 *MATTHEW THORNTON, NEW HAMPSHIRE* Painful beyond expression, gentlemen, have been those scenes of blood and devastation which the barbarous cruelty of British troops have placed before our eyes. Duty to God, to ourselves, to posterity; these ends forced by the cries of slaughtered innocence have urged us to take up arms in our own defense!

34 *WILLIAM WHIPPLE, NEW HAMPSHIRE* Gentlemen, nothing less than the fate of America depends on the virtue of her sons, and if we do not have virtue enough to support the most glorious cause ever human beings were engaged in, we don't deserve the blessings of freedom!

35 *THOMAS JEFFERSON, VIRGINIA* Truly, our cause is just. Our union is perfect. Our internal resources are great, and, if necessary, foreign assistance is undoubtedly attainable. The arms we have been compelled by our enemies to assume we will, in defiance of every hazard, with unabating firmness and perseverance, employ for the preservation of our liberties; being with one mind resolved to die freemen rather than live slaves!

36 *JOHN ADAMS, MASSACHUSETTS* Friends, distinguished gentlemen: Sink or swim, live or die, survive or perish, I give my hand and my heart to this vote. It is true, indeed, that in the beginning we aimed not at independence. But there's a divinity that shapes our ends. Why, then, should we defer the Declaration? You and I, indeed, may rue it. We may not live to see the time when this Declaration shall be made good. We may die: die colonists, die slaves, die, it

may be, ignominiously and on the scaffold.

Be it so. Be it so.

If it be the pleasure of Heaven that my country shall require the poor offering of my life, the victim shall be ready; but while I do live, let me have a country, or at least the hope of a country, and that of a free country.

But whatever may be our fate, be assured that this Declaration will stand. It may cost treasure, and it may cost blood, but it will stand, and it will richly compensate for both.

Through the thick gloom of the present, I see the brightness of the future as the sun in heaven. We shall make this a glorious, an immortal, day. When we are in our graves, our children will honor it. They will celebrate it with thanksgiving, with festivity, with bonfires, and illuminations.

Before God, I believe the hour is come. My judgment approves this measure, and my whole heart is in it. All that I have, and all that I am, and all that I hope, in this life, I am now ready here to stake upon it; and I leave off as I began, that live or die, survive or perish, I am for the Declaration. It is my living sentiment, and by the blessing of God, it shall be my dying sentiment. Independence now! Independence forever!

37 *JOHN HANCOCK, MASSACHUSETTS* I urge you, Gentlemen, by all that is dear, by all that is honorable, by all that is sacred, not only that you pray, but also that you act!!!

SCRIBE The patriots sought a unanimous declaration of the Thirteen Colonies. Each of the colonies had a majority in favor of independence—except Delaware. Divided between the two delegates present, an urgent note was sent to the third delegate, Caesar Rodney, imploring him to return to Philadelphia at once to cast the deciding vote for a unanimous independence.

38 *WILLIAM FRANK* Rodney hastened from his farm on St. Jones Neck. There wasn't an hour to waste. A lone rider, suffering from a serious facial cancer and afflicted with asthma, was headed for Philadelphia.

39 *WILLIAM FRANK* It was an agonizing eighteen-hour, eighty-mile ride through the summer's heat and into the night. He rode despite the thunderstorm and torrential rain, over dirt roads choked with mud, across rickety bridges spanning swollen streams, and over slippery cobblestone streets in towns and cities. He rode northward, with the Delaware River on his right and the sweeping farms of the Talleys, the Grubbs, and allied families on his left. He passed old taverns, such as the Practical Farmer near Grubb's Landing, on through Upland, until he reached Gray's Ferry outside Philadelphia. From there, Rodney followed the established post route to the State House. He tarried only briefly for some food and drink and to change horses.

40 *WILLIAM FRANK* Caesar Rodney arrived at what would become known as Independence Hall in the afternoon of July 2. McKean, his fellow Delaware delegate, was anxiously waiting for him.

41 *THOMAS MCKEAN* Rodney was tired, dusty, and covered with mud. He was booted and spurred. Together, we entered the hall and went quickly into the chamber where the debate on Lee's resolution was nearing a close. 42 *CAESAR RODNEY, DELAWARE* Gentlemen, as I believe the voice of my constituents and of all sensible and honest men is in favor of independence, my own judgment concurs with them. I vote for independence!

43 JOHN ADAMS And thus the greatest question was decided which ever was debated in America; and a greater perhaps never was, nor will be, decided among men. A resolution was passed without one dissenting colony "that these United Colonies are, and of right ought to be, free and independent states!" *SCRIBE* And thanks to the midnight ride of Caesar Rodney, it was now, *44 DECLARATION OF INDEPENDENCE* the unanimous Declaration of the thirteen United States of America.

45 BENJAMIN RUSH July 4, 1776: A pensive and awful silence pervaded the house as we were called up, one after another, to the table of the President of Congress to subscribe what was believed by many to be our own death warrants. The silence and the gloom of the morning were interrupted only for a moment by Colonel Harrison of Virginia, who said to Mr. Eldridge Gerry at the table: "I shall have a great advantage over you, Mr. Gerry, when we are all hung for what we are now doing. From the size and weight of my body I shall die in a few minutes, but from the lightness of your body you will dance in the air an hour or two before you are dead."

46 BENJAMIN FRANKLIN I would say, Gentlemen, we must all hang together, or assuredly, we shall all hang separately.

SCRIBE "There!" Mr. Hancock said, as he stood and pointed at his signature, *47 JOHN HANCOCK* "His Majesty can now read my name without glasses, and he can double the reward on my head!"

48 BENJAMIN RUSH 'Tis done. We have become a nation.

49 SAMUEL ADAMS My friends, we have fled from the political Sodom; let us not look back lest we perish and become a monument of infamy and derision to the world. *50 SAMUEL ADAMS* For we have this day restored the Sovereign, to whom alone men ought to be obedient. He reigns in heaven, and with a propitious eye beholds His subjects assuming that freedom of thought and dignity of self-direction which He bestowed on them. And, brethren and fellow countrymen, if it was ever granted to mortals to trace the designs of providence to this day and interpret its manifestations in favor of their cause, we may with humility of soul, cry out, "Not unto us, not unto us, but to Thy name be the praise!"

51 *JAMES MONROE* The Declaration of Independence confirmed in form what had existed before in substance. It announced to the world that new states possessed and exercised complete sovereignty which they were resolved to maintain; 52 *JOHN QUINCY ADAMS* that a new civilization had come, a new spirit had arisen on this side of the Atlantic more advanced and more developed in its regard for the rights of the individual than that which characterized the Old World; that life in a new and open country had aspirations which could not be realized in any subordinate position; that it had been decreed by the very laws of human nature; and that man everywhere has an unconquerable desire to be the master of his own destiny!

SCRIBE Forty-five years after signing the declaration, John Adams reflected on the meaning of that first Independence Day: 53 *JOHN ADAMS* And now, friends and countrymen, if the wise and learned philosophers of the elder world should find their hearts disposed to inquire what has America done for the benefit of mankind, let our answer be this:

America, with the same voice which spoke herself into existence as a nation, proclaimed to mankind the inextinguishable rights of human nature and the only lawful foundations of government. America, in the assembly of nations since her admission among them, has invariably, though often fruitlessly, held forth to them the hand of honest friendship, of equal freedom, and of generous reciprocity.

Wherever the standard of freedom and independence has been or shall be unfurled, there will her heart, her benedictions, and her prayers be.

She goes not abroad, in search of monsters to destroy. She is the well-wisher to the freedom and independence of all.

She is the champion and vindicator only of her own. She will commend the general cause by the countenance of her voice and the benignant sympathy of her example.

America's glory is not dominion, but liberty. Her march is the march of the mind. She has a spear and a shield, but the motto upon her shield is: "Freedom, Independence, Peace." This has been her declaration; *SCRIBE* this motionless scroll—54 *DANIEL WEBSTER* this will be the most powerful of speakers. Its speech will be of civil and religious liberty. It will speak of patriotism and of courage. It will speak of the moral improvement and elevation of mankind. Ingenuous youth will gather round it while they speak to each other of the glorious events with which it is connected and exclaim, "Thank God I also am an American!"

Chapter Nine
Republic

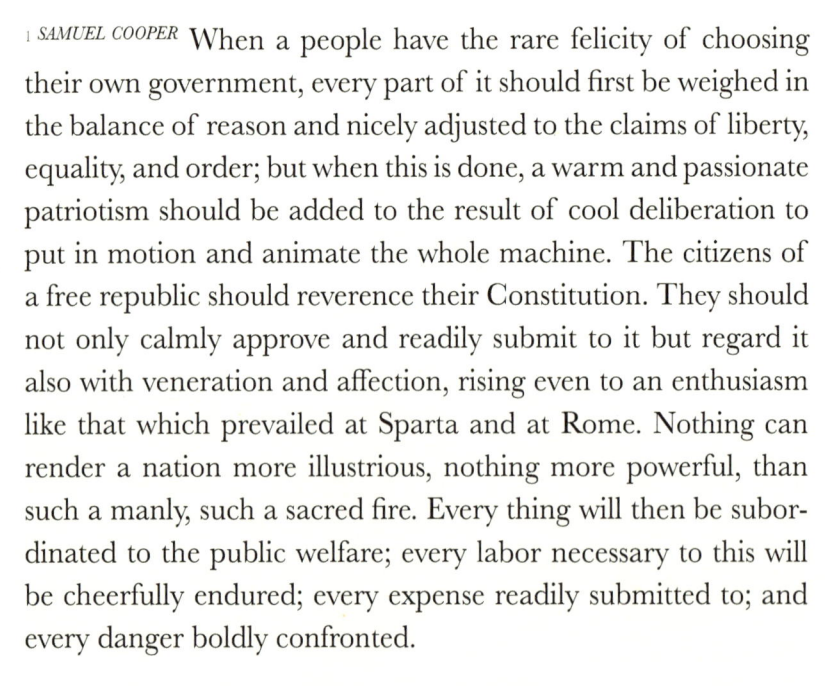

1 *SAMUEL COOPER* When a people have the rare felicity of choosing their own government, every part of it should first be weighed in the balance of reason and nicely adjusted to the claims of liberty, equality, and order; but when this is done, a warm and passionate patriotism should be added to the result of cool deliberation to put in motion and animate the whole machine. The citizens of a free republic should reverence their Constitution. They should not only calmly approve and readily submit to it but regard it also with veneration and affection, rising even to an enthusiasm like that which prevailed at Sparta and at Rome. Nothing can render a nation more illustrious, nothing more powerful, than such a manly, such a sacred fire. Every thing will then be subordinated to the public welfare; every labor necessary to this will be cheerfully endured; every expense readily submitted to; and every danger boldly confronted.

May this heavenly flame animate all orders of men in the state. May it catch from bosom to bosom, and the glow be universal. May a double portion of it inhabit the breasts of our civil rulers and impart a luster to them like that which sat upon the face of Moses when he came down from the holy mountain with the tables of the Hebrew constitution in his hand. Thus will they sustain, with true dignity, the first honors; the first marks of esteem and confidence; and the first public employments bestowed by this new nation in which they this day appear. [2] *JOHN ADAMS* Thus will they acknowledge that the safety and prosperity of nations ultimately and essentially depend on the protection and the blessing of Almighty God. [3] *JOHN ADAMS* Thus will they submit to the indispensable duty which the people owe to Him, to the promotion of that morality and piety without which social happiness can not exist, nor the blessings of a free government be enjoyed.

[4] *F.W. ROBERTSON* It is a common saying that religion has nothing to do with politics, and particularly there is a strong feeling current against all interference with politics by the ministers of religion. But to say that religion has nothing to do with politics is to assert that which is simply false. It were as wise to say that the atmosphere has nothing to do with the principles of architecture. Religion is the vital air of every question. Directly, it determines nothing; indirectly, it conditions every problem that can arise.

[5] *NOAH WEBSTER* When you become entitled to exercise the right of voting for public officers, let it be impressed on your mind that God commands you to choose for rulers, "just men who will rule in the fear of God." [6] *SAMUEL COOKE* For rulers must not forget that they ruleth over *men*: men who are of the same species with himself, and by nature, equal; men who are the offspring of God, and alike formed after His glorious image; men of like passions and feelings with himself; and as men, in the sight of their common Creator, of equal importance.

[7] *SAMUEL COOPER* You must choose men who have steadily acted upon the noble principles on which the frame of our government now rests; men who have generously neglected their private interest in an ardent pursuit of that of the public; men who will put their fortunes and their lives to no small hazard in fixing the basis of

our freedom and honor; and men who—casting up a thankful eye to Heaven, and freely chosen by ourselves—come forth at the call of their country from the midst of us.

8 *WILLIAM O. DOUGLAS* Our society, unlike most in the world, presupposes that freedom and liberty are in a frame of reference which makes the individual, not government, the keeper of his tastes, beliefs, and ideas; 9 *SAMUEL ADAMS* that He who made all men hath made the truths necessary to human happiness obvious to all; 10 *SAMUEL COOKE* that men are moral agents, obliged to act according to the natural and evident relation of things and the rank they bear in God's creation; 11 *THOMAS JEFFERSON* that every man, and every body of men on earth, possesses the right of self-government; 12 *EDMUND BURKE* that no name, no power, no function, no artificial institution whatsoever, can make of men other than God, Nature, education, and their habits of life have made them.

13 *DANIEL WEBSTER* Liberty exists in proportion to wholesome restraint: the more restraint on others to keep off from us, the more liberty we have. 14 *DANIEL WEBSTER* For there is no happiness—there is no enjoyment of life—unless a man can say when he rises in the morning, "I shall be subject to the decision of no unwise judge today."

15 *WILLIAM O. DOUGLAS* This is the philosophy of the First Amendment. This is the article of faith that sets us apart from most nations in the world.

16 *DANIEL WEBSTER* You have been taught to regard a representative of the people as a sentinel on the watchtower of liberty; 17 *EDMUND BURKE* that it is better to cherish virtue and humanity by leaving much to free will than to attempt to make men mere machines and instruments of a political benevolence; 18 *PATRICK HENRY*

that you are not to inquire how your trade may be increased, nor how you are to become a great and powerful people, but to inquire how your liberties can be secured, for liberty ought to be the direct end of your government.

19 EDMUND BURKE Sadly, there are leaders who choose to make themselves bidders at an auction of popularity. They become flatterers instead of legislators; the instruments, not the guides, of the people. 20 ALEXIS DE TOCQUEVILLE If any principled man should happen to propose a scheme of liberty, soberly limited and defined with proper qualifications, he will be immediately outbid by these men, who will produce something more splendidly popular.

21 FRÉDÉRIC BASTIAT These are men who compare the nation to a parched piece of land and the tax to a life-giving rain. So be it. But they should ask themselves where this rain comes from, and whether it is not precisely the tax that draws the moisture from the soil and dries it up. They should also ask themselves whether the soil receives more of this precious water from the rain than it loses by the evaporation?

22 LUDWIG VON MISES Once the principle is admitted that it is the duty of the government to protect the individual against his own foolishness, no serious objections can be advanced against further encroachments. 23 FRÉDÉRIC BASTIAT For as long as these ideas prevail, it is clear that the responsibility of government is enormous. Good fortune and bad fortune, wealth and poverty, equality and inequality, virtue and vice—all then depend upon political administration.

24 ALEXIS DE TOCQUEVILLE What good does it do me if an ever-watchful authority—who keeps an eye out to ensure that my pleasures will be tranquil and races ahead of me to ward off all danger, sparing

me the need even to think about such things—if that authority, even as it removes the smallest thorns from my path, is also absolute master of my liberty and my life? What good if it monopolizes vitality and existence to such a degree that when it languishes, everything around it must also languish; when it sleeps, everything must also sleep; and when it dies, everything must also perish?

SCRIBE Cicero warned the Roman Republic of their impending doom when he said: [25] *CICERO* The budget should be balanced, the treasury refilled, public debt reduced, the arrogance of officialdom tempered and controlled, and the assistance to foreign lands curtailed, lest Rome become bankrupt. [26] *TEDDY ROOSEVELT* Yet the Roman Republic fell, not because of the ambition of Caesar or Augustus, but because it had already long ceased to be in any real sense a republic at all. When the sturdy Roman plebeian—who lived by his own labor, who voted without reward according to his own convictions, and who with his fellows formed in war the terrible Roman legion—had been changed into an idle creature—who craved nothing in life save the gratification of a thirst for vapid excitement, who was fed by the state, and who directly or indirectly sold his vote to the highest bidder—then the end of the republic was at hand, and nothing could save it.

[27] *JOHN MILTON* Nations grow corrupt, love bondage more than liberty—bondage with ease than strenuous liberty. [28] *THOMAS JEFFERSON* This is the tendency of all human governments. As a departure from principle in one instance becomes a precedent for another until the bulk of society is reduced to be mere automatons of misery. The forehorse of this frightful team is public debt. Taxation follows that, and in its train, wretchedness and oppression.

[29] *ALEXIS DE TOCQUEVILLE* Our contemporaries are constantly wracked by two warring passions: They feel the need to be led and the

desire to remain free. Unable to destroy either of these contrary instincts, they seek to satisfy both at once. They imagine a single, omnipotent, tutelary power, but one that is elected by the citizens. They combine centralization with popular sovereignty. This gives them some respite. They console themselves for being treated as wards by imagining that they have chosen their own protectors. Each individual, thus, allows himself to be clapped in chains because the other end of the chain is held not by a man or a class but by the people themselves.

[30] *FISHER AMES* It is the almost universal mistake of our countrymen that democracy would be mild and safe in America. They charge the horrid excesses of France not so much to human nature, which will never act better when the restraints of government, morals, and religion are thrown off, but to the characteristic cruelty and wickedness of the Jacobins. The truth is—and let it humble our pride—the most ferocious of all animals, when his passions are roused to fury and are uncontrolled, is man; and of all governments, the worst is that which never fails to excite, but was never found to restrain those passions—that is, democracy.

[31] *JOHN ADAMS* There is nothing in which mankind have been more unanimous, yet nothing can be inferred from it more than this: that the multitude have always been credulous, and the few, artful. [32] *POLYBIUS* When, in their senseless mania for reputation, the rich have made the populace ready and greedy to receive bribes, the virtue of democracy is destroyed, and it is transformed into a government of violence and the strong hand. The mob—habituated to feed at the expense of others and to have its hopes of a livelihood in the property of its neighbors—as soon as it has got a leader sufficiently ambitious and daring, comes to tumultuous assemblies, massacres, banishments, and redivisions of land until

after losing all trace of civilization, it has once more found a master and a despot.

33 *ALEXIS DE TOCQUEVILLE* A democracy leads men unceasingly to multiply the privileges of the federal government and to circumscribe the rights of private persons, often sacrificed without regret and almost always violated without remorse. Men become less and less attached to private rights, just when it is most necessary to retain and defend what little remains of them.

34 *ALEXANDER FRASER TYTLER* Democracy cannot exist as a permanent form of government. It can only exist until the voters discover that they can vote themselves largess of the public treasury. From that time on, the majority always votes for the candidates promising the most benefits from the public treasury, with the results that a democracy always collapses over loose fiscal policy, always followed by a dictatorship.

35 *ALEXANDER FRASER TYTLER* The average age of the world's greatest civilizations has been two hundred years. These nations have progressed through this sequence: from bondage to spiritual faith; from spiritual faith to great courage; from great courage to liberty; from liberty to abundance; from abundance to selfishness; from selfishness to complacency; from complacency to apathy; from apathy to dependence; and from dependency, back again to bondage.

36 *THOMAS JEFFERSON* I am convinced that a republic is the only form of government which is not eternally at open or secret war with the rights of mankind. 37 *JOHN ADAMS* For the true idea of a republic is "an empire of laws, and not of men;" a particular arrangement of the powers of society best contrived to secure an impartial and exact execution of the law; 38 *THOMAS PAINE* a constitution

that defines and limits the powers of the government it creates; 39 *GEORGE WASHINGTON* a reciprocal check in the exercise of political power, dividing and distributing it into different depositories.

40 *THOMAS JEFFERSON* My friends, it is not by the consolidation or concentration of powers, but by their distribution that good government is effected. Were not this great country already divided into states, that division must be made, that each might do for itself what concerns itself directly and what it can so much better do than a distant authority. It is by this partition of cares, descending in gradation from general to particular, that the mass of human affairs may be best managed for the good and prosperity of all.

41 *THOMAS JEFFERSON* What has destroyed liberty and the rights of man in every government which has ever existed under the sun? The generalizing and concentrating all cares and powers into one body. 42 *THOMAS JEFFERSON* The way to have good and safe government is not to trust it all to one, but to divide it among the many, distributing to every one exactly the functions he is competent to. Let the national government be entrusted with the defense of the nation and its foreign and federal relations; 43 *THOMAS JEFFERSON* let it serve as a barrier against foreign foes; and to watch the border of every state, so that no external hand may intrude or disturb the exercise of the self-government reserved to itself.

44 *THOMAS JEFFERSON* Let the state governments be entrusted with the civil rights, laws, police, and administration of what concerns the state generally; the counties, with the local concerns of the counties, and each ward† or district the interests within itself. For it is by dividing and subdividing these republics until it ends in the administration of every man's farm by himself, by placing

---

† Ward: to guard.

under every one what his own eye may superintend, that good government is effected; 45 *THOMAS JEFFERSON* each to take care of what lies within its local bounds; each to manage minuter details; each to be governed by its individual proprietor; 46 *JOHN ADAMS* each to attain the ends to which it was designed.

47 *THOMAS JEFFERSON* I consider the foundation of the Constitution as laid on this ground: That "the powers not delegated to the United States by the Constitution, nor prohibited by it to the States, are reserved to the States respectively, or to the people"; 48 *JOHN ADAMS* that the general government must not be allowed to override the more fundamental claims of the states; 49 *FISHER AMES* that the states are the safeguard and ornament of the Constitution, representing the local interests of the people; affording a shelter against the abuse of power; and avenging our violated rights.

50 *THOMAS JEFFERSON* My friends, were we directed from Washington when to sow and when to reap, we should soon want bread. 51 *JOHN ADAMS* But a government of our own choice, managed by persons whom we love, revere, and can confide in; this has charms in it for which men will fight.

52 *JOHN MARSHALL* No political dreamer was ever wild enough to think of breaking down the lines which separate the states and compounding the American people into one common mass. 53 *ABEL UPSHUR* For the general government is the creature of the states. It is not a party to the Constitution but the result of it, the creation of that agreement which was made by the states as parties. 54 *JAMES MADISON* Thus, in the sovereign capacity of the states, it follows of necessity, that there can be no tribunal above their authority to decide in the last resort whether the compact made by them be violated and whether such questions are of sufficient magnitude to require their interposition. 55 *ABEL UPSHUR* Should the

general government, a mere agent entrusted with limited powers for certain specific objects, be permitted to judge the extent of its own powers when that same government is always in subordination to the authority by whom its powers were conferred?

56 *JOHN ADAMS* Friends, I have come to the conclusion that one useless man is a disgrace, that two become a law firm, and that three or more become a congress. 57 *DANIEL WEBSTER* Now is the time when men work quietly in the fields and women weep softly in the kitchen: The legislature is in session, and no man's property is safe. 58 *THOMAS PAINE* Sadly, our calamity is only heightened by reflecting that we furnish the means by which we suffer.

59 *REPRESENTATIVE DAVY CROCKETT IN A SPEECH TO CONGRESS* When riding one day in a part of my district in which I was more of a stranger than any other, I saw a man in a field plowing and coming toward the road. I gauged my gait so that we should meet as he came to the fence. As he came up, I spoke to the man. He replied politely, but, as I thought, rather coldly. I began: "Well, friend, I am one of those unfortunate beings called candidates, and . . .

HORATIO BUNCE Yes, I know you; you are Colonel Crockett. I have seen you once before and voted for you the last time you were elected. I suppose you are out electioneering now, but you had better not waste your time or mine. I shall not vote for you again.

DAVY CROCKETT Sir, That is a sockdolager.† I beg you tell what is the matter.

HORATIO BUNCE Well, Colonel, it is hardly worthwhile to waste time or words upon it. I do not see how it can be mended, but you gave a vote last winter which shows that either you have not capacity to

---

† Sockdologer: A forceful blow.

understand the Constitution or that you are wanting in the honesty and firmness to be guided by it. In either case, you are not the man to represent me. But I beg your pardon for expressing it in that way. I intend by it only to say that your understanding of the Constitution is very different from mine. I believe you to be honest. But an understanding of the Constitution different from mine I cannot overlook, because the Constitution, to be worth anything, must be held sacred and rigidly observed in all its provisions. The man who wields power and misinterprets it is the more dangerous the more honest he is.

DAVY CROCKETT I admit the truth of all you say, but there must be some mistake about it, for I do not remember that I gave any vote last winter upon any Constitutional question.

HORATIO BUNCE No, Colonel, there's no mistake. Though I live here in the backwoods and seldom go from home, I take the papers from Washington and read very carefully all the proceedings of Congress. My papers say that last winter you voted for a bill to appropriate $20,000 to some sufferers by a fire in Georgetown. Is that true?'

DAVY CROCKETT Well, my friend; I may as well own up. You have got me there. But certainly nobody will complain that a great and rich country like ours should give the insignificant sum of $20,000 to relieve its suffering women and children, particularly with a full and overflowing treasury, and I am sure if you had been there, you would have done just as I did.

HORATIO BUNCE It is not the amount, Colonel, that I complain of; it is the principle. In the first place, the government ought to have in the treasury no more than enough for its legitimate purposes. But that has nothing to do with the question. The power of collecting and disbursing money at pleasure is the most dangerous power that can be entrusted to man, particularly under our system of collecting revenue by a tariff, which reaches every man in the country no matter how poor he may be, and the poorer he is, the more he pays in proportion to his means. What is worse, it presses upon him without his knowledge where the weight centers, for there is not a man in the United States who can ever guess how much he pays to the government.

So you see, that while you are contributing to relieve one, you are drawing it from thousands who are even worse off than he. If you had the right to give anything, the amount was simply a matter of discretion with you, and you had as much right to give $20,000,000 as $20,000. If you have the right to give to one, you have the right to give to all; and, as the Constitution neither defines charity nor stipulates the amount, you are at liberty to give to any and everything which you may believe, or profess to believe, is a charity, and to any amount you may think proper. You will very easily perceive what a wide door this would open for fraud and corruption and favoritism on the one hand, and for robbing the people on the other.

No, Colonel, Congress has no right to give charity. Individual members may give as much of their own money as they please, but they have no right to touch a dollar of the public money for that purpose. If twice as many houses had been burned in this county as in Georgetown, neither you nor any other member of Congress would have thought of appropriating a dollar for our relief. There are about two hundred and forty members of Congress. If they had shown their sympathy for the sufferers by contributing each one week's pay, it would have made over $13,000. There are plenty of wealthy men in and around Washington who could have given $20,000 without depriving themselves of even a luxury of life. The congressmen chose to keep their own money. The people about Washington, no doubt, applauded you for relieving them from the necessity of giving by giving what was not yours to give. The people have delegated to Congress, by the Constitution, the power to do certain things. To do these, it is authorized to collect and pay moneys and for nothing else. Everything beyond this is usurpation and a violation of the Constitution.

So you see, Colonel, you have violated the Constitution in what I consider a vital point. It is a precedent fraught with danger to the country, for when Congress once begins to stretch its power beyond the limits of the Constitution, there is no limit to it and no security for the people. I have no doubt you acted honestly, but that does not make it any better, except as far as you are personally concerned, and you see that I cannot vote for you.

DAVY CROCKETT My friend, I feel streaked.[†] I am fully convinced that you are right. You hit the nail upon the head when you said I had not sense enough to understand the Constitution. I intended to be guided by it and thought I had studied it fully. I have heard many speeches in Congress about the powers of Congress, but what you have said here at your plow has got more hard, sound sense in it than all the fine speeches I ever heard.

If I had ever taken the view of it that you have, I would have put my head into the fire before I would have given that vote; and if you will forgive me and vote for me again, if I *ever* vote for another unconstitutional law, I wish I may be shot.

HORATIO BUNCE Yes, Colonel, you have sworn to that once before, but

---

† Streaked: Physically upset.

I will trust you again upon one condition. You say that you are convinced that your vote was wrong. Your acknowledgment of it will do more good than beating you for it. If, as you go around the district, you will tell people about this vote, and that you are satisfied it was wrong, I will not only vote for you, but I will do what I can to keep down opposition, and, perhaps, I may exert some little influence in that way.

DAVY CROCKETT If I don't, I wish I may be shot; and to convince you that I am in earnest in what I say, I will come back this way in a week or ten days, and if you will get a gathering of the people, I will make a speech to them. Get up a barbecue, and I will pay for it.

HORATIO BUNCE No, Colonel, we are not rich people in this section, but we have plenty of provisions to contribute for a barbecue and some to spare for those who have none. The push of crops will be over in a few days, and we can then afford a day for a barbecue.

DAVY CROCKETT I will be there. But one thing more before I say goodbye. I must know your name.

HORATIO BUNCE My name is Bunce.

DAVY CROCKETT Not Horatio Bunce?

HORATIO BUNCE Yes.

DAVY CROCKETT Well, Mr. Bunce, I never saw you before, though you say you have seen me, but I know you very well. I am glad I have met you and very proud that I may hope to have you for my friend. You must let me shake your hand before I go.

DAVY CROCKETT My friends, it was one of the luckiest hits of my life that I met that man. He mingled but little with the public, but was widely known for his remarkable intelligence, incorruptible integrity, and heart brimful and running over with kindness and benevolence, which showed themselves not only in words but in acts. He was the oracle of the whole country around him, and his fame extended far beyond the circle of his immediate acquaintance.

DAVY CROCKETT At the appointed time I was at his house, having told our conversation to every crowd I had met. In fact, I found that it gave the people an interest and a confidence in me stronger than I had ever seen manifest before. Though I was considerably fatigued when I reached the home of Mr. Bunce, and under ordinary circumstances should have gone early to bed, I kept him up until midnight, talking about the principles and affairs of government and got more real, true knowledge of them than I had got all my life before.

DAVY CROCKETT I have told you gentlemen how Mr. Bunce converted me politically. He came nearer converting me religiously than I had ever been before. He did not make a very good Christian of me, as you know; but he has wrought upon my feelings a reverence for its purifying and elevating power such as I had never felt before. I have known and seen much of him since, for I respect him—no, that is not the word—I reverence and love him more than any living man, and I go to see him two or three times every year. And I will say to you gentlemen, if every one who professes to be a Christian lived and acted and enjoyed it as he does, the religion of Christ would take the world by storm.

DAVY CROCKETT But to return to my story: The next morning we went to the barbecue, and, to my surprise, found about a thousand people there. They gathered up around a stand that had been erected. I told the crowd gathered about the fire and my vote for the appropriation as I have told it to you, and then told them why I was satisfied it was wrong. I closed by saying:

DAVY CROCKETT Fellow citizens, I present myself before you today feeling like a new man. My eyes have lately been opened to truths which ignorance or prejudice, or both, had heretofore hidden from my view. I feel that I can today offer you the ability to render you more valuable service than I have ever been able to render before. I am here today more for the purpose of acknowledging my error than to seek your votes. That I should make this acknowledgment is due to myself as well as to you. Whether you will vote for me is a matter for your consideration only. And now, fellow citizens, it remains only for me to tell you that most of the speech you have listened to with so much interest was simply a repetition of the arguments by which your neighbor, Mr. Bunce, convinced me of my error. And now I hope he is satisfied with his convert and that he will get up here and tell you so.

DAVY CROCKETT Mr. Bunce came upon the stand and said to the crowd:

HORATIO BUNCE Fellow citizens, it affords me great pleasure to comply with the request of Colonel Crockett. I have always considered him a thoroughly honest man, and I am satisfied that he will faithfully perform all that he has promised you today.

DAVY CROCKETT I am not much given to tears, Gentlemen, but I was taken with a choking then and felt some big drops rolling down my cheeks. And I tell you now that the remembrance of those few words spoken by such a man, and the honest, hearty shout they produced from the crowd, is worth more to me than all the honors I have received and all the reputation I have ever made, or ever shall make, as a member of Congress.

SCRIBE Congressman Crockett returned to his seat.

60 *JAMES MADISON* If it be asked, what is to be the consequence, in case Congress shall misconstrue this part of the Constitution and exercise powers not warranted by its true meaning, I answer: the same as if they should misconstrue or enlarge any other power vested in them; as if the general power had been reduced to particulars and any one of these were to be violated; the same, in short, as if the state legislatures should violate their respective constitutional authorities. In the first instance, the success of the usurpation will depend on the executive and judiciary departments, which are to expound and give effect to the legislative acts; and in the last resort, a remedy must be obtained from the people who can, by the election of more faithful representatives, annul the acts of the usurpers.

61 *G.K. CHESTERTON* My friends, government has become ungovernable; that is, it cannot leave off governing. Law has become lawless; that is, it cannot see where laws should stop. The chief feature of our time is the meekness of the mob and the madness of the government. 62 *JOHN DICKINSON* For no free people ever existed, or can ever exist, without keeping the purse strings in their own hands. Where this is the case, they have a constitutional check upon the administration which may thereby be brought into order without violence. But when such a power is not lodged in the people, oppression proceeds uncontrolled in its career until the governed, transported into rage, seek redress in the midst of blood and confusion.

63 *THOMAS JEFFERSON* When the representative body have lost the confidence of their constituents; when they have notoriously made sale of their most valuable rights; when they have assumed to themselves powers which the people never put into their hands; then indeed their continuing in office becomes dangerous to the state

and calls for an exercise of the power of dissolution. [64] *DANIEL WEBSTER* For who will show me any Constitutional injunction which makes it the duty of the American people to surrender everything valuable in life, and even life itself, whenever the purposes of an ambitious and mischievous government may require it.

[65] *ANONYMOUS PATRIOT* The encroachment upon the rights and property of citizens resembles the relentless surge of mighty waters breaching ancient mounds: initially slow and unalarming, but swiftly escalating into a torrential current, ultimately resulting in deluge and devastation. Consider the oak tree, once an acorn nestled within the earth's depths, now stretching its branches toward the mountains, casting shadows over valleys. Similarly, the insidious grip of government slavery, which recently took root among us, has already spread across the land—its tendrils reaching toward the ocean and its limbs extending to the rivers.

Under its cover, unclean and voracious creatures find refuge and sustenance, while the very shade it casts withers the green herb, and its roots poison the once fertile ground. The winds that rustle its branches carry not life, but pestilence and death.

Let us heed this warning, my friends, and stand vigilant against the creeping darkness that threatens to engulf our liberties and fracture our society. For like the oak, we must remain rooted in justice lest we become mere shadows of our former selves, swept away by the tempests of history.

[66] *JOHN ADAMS* Our Constitution is founded—'tis bottomed and grounded—on the knowledge and good sense of the people. The very ground of our liberties is the freedom of elections. [67] *ALEXANDER HAMILTON* For the true principle of a republic is that the people should choose whom they please to govern them.

[68] *ALEXANDER HAMILTON* This great source of free government and popular election should be perfectly pure. [69] *JOHN ADAMS* For corruption in elections has heretofore destroyed all elective governments. What regulations or precautions may be devised to prevent it in future, I am content to leave to posterity to consider.

Chapter Ten
Posterity

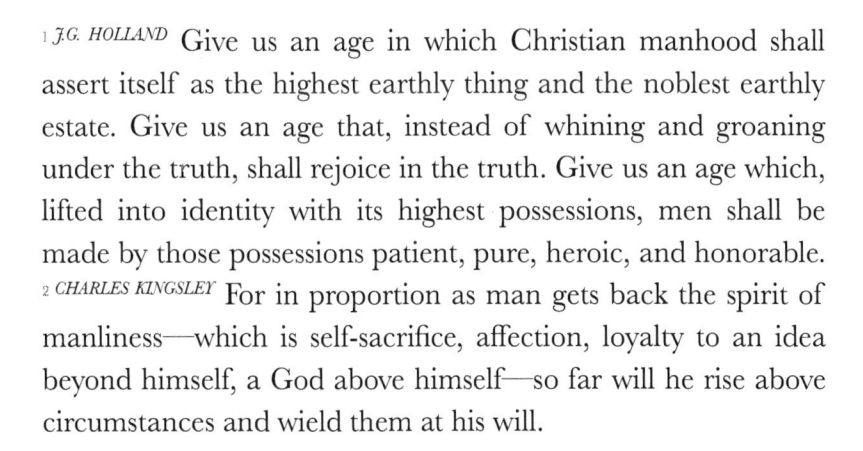

[1] *J.G. HOLLAND* Give us an age in which Christian manhood shall assert itself as the highest earthly thing and the noblest earthly estate. Give us an age that, instead of whining and groaning under the truth, shall rejoice in the truth. Give us an age which, lifted into identity with its highest possessions, men shall be made by those possessions patient, pure, heroic, and honorable. [2] *CHARLES KINGSLEY* For in proportion as man gets back the spirit of manliness—which is self-sacrifice, affection, loyalty to an idea beyond himself, a God above himself—so far will he rise above circumstances and wield them at his will.

[3] *THOMAS JEFFERSON* It is fortitude that teaches us to meet and surmount difficulties, not to fly from them like cowards; and to fly, too, in vain, for they will meet and arrest us at every turn of our road. [4] *SENECA* The greatest man is he who chooses the right with the most invincible resolution; who resists the sorest temptation from within and without; who bears the heaviest burdens cheerfully; who is calmest in storms and most fearless under menaces and frowns; and whose reliance on truth, on virtue, and on God is most unfaltering.

[5] *GEORGE BANCROFT* In America, a new people had risen up without a king, or princes, or nobles, knowing nothing of tithes and little

of landlords, the plough being in the hands of the freeholders of the soil. They were more sincerely religious, better educated, and of purer morals than the men of any former republic. By calm meditation and friendly councils, they had prepared a Constitution which in the union of freedom with strength and order, excelled every one known before, and which secured itself against violence and revolution by providing a peaceful method for every needed reform.

6 *THOMAS JEFFERSON* My friends, the station which we occupy among the nations of the earth is honorable, but awful. We are trusted with the destinies of this solitary republic of the world, the only monument of human rights, and the sole depository of the sacred fire of freedom and self-government, from hence it is to be lighted up in other regions of the earth, if other regions of the earth shall ever become susceptible of its benign influence.

7 *HENRY ARMITT BROWN* The years that are before us are a virgin page. We can inscribe them as we will. The future of our country rests upon us. The happiness of posterity depends on us. The fate of humanity may be in our hands. That pleading voice, choked with the sobs of ages, which has so often spoken to deaf ears, is lifted up to us. It asks us to be brave, benevolent, consistent, and true to the teachings of our history, proving "divine descent by worth divine." It asks us to be virtuous, building up public virtue upon private worth, seeking that righteousness which exalteth nations. It asks us to be patriotic, loving our country before all other things, making her happiness our happiness; her honor, ours; and her fame, our own. It asks us in the name of charity; in the name of freedom; in the name of God.

8 *JOHN DICKINSON* My fellow citizens, it is not our duty to leave wealth to our children, but it is our duty to leave liberty to them, to

transmit to our posterity that liberty which we received from our ancestors. No infamy, iniquity, or cruelty can exceed our own if we—born and educated in a country of freedom, entitled to its blessings and knowing their value, pusillanimously[†] deserting the post assigned us by divine providence—surrender succeeding generations to a condition of wretchedness.

[9 SIMEON HOWARD] They are not here to act their part. A concern for them is a debt which we owe for the care which our progenitors took for us. [10 SIMEON HOWARD] For heaven has made us their guardians and entrusted to our care their liberty, honor, and happiness. If the present inhabitants of a country submit to slavery, slavery is the inheritance which they will leave to their children. And who that has the heart of a father, or even the common feelings of humanity, can think without horror of being the means of subjecting unborn millions to the iron scepter of tyranny?

[11 MERCY OTIS WARREN] On these shores, freedom has planted her standard, dipped in the purple tide that flowed from the veins of her martyred heroes; and here, every uncorrupted American yet hopes to see it supported by the vigor, the justice, the wisdom, and the unanimity of the people, in spite of the deep-laid plots, the secret intrigues, or the bold effrontery of those interested and avaricious adventurers for place who, intoxicated with the ideas of distinction and preferment, have prostrated every worthy principle beneath the shrine of ambition.

[12 MERCY OTIS WARREN] They tell us republicanism is dwindled into theory, that we are incapable of enjoying our liberties, that we must have a master. [13 JOSIAH QUINCY] Sanctified by authority and armed with power, error and usurpation they thus bid defiance

---

[†] Pusillanimously: lacking courage and resolution.

to truth and right, while the bulk of mankind sit gazing at the monster of their own creation: a monster to which their follies and vices gave origin, and their depravity and cowardice continue it's existence.

14 *MERCY OTIS WARREN* When patriotism is discountenanced and public virtue becomes the ridicule of the sycophant—when every man of liberality, firmness, and penetration who cannot lick the hand stretched out to oppress is deemed an enemy to the State—then is the gulf of despotism set open and the grades to slavery, though rapid, are scarce perceptible—then genius drags heavily its iron chain, science is neglected, and real merit flies to the shades for security from reproach—then the mind becomes enervated and the national character sinks to a kind of apathy with only energy sufficient to curse the breast that gave it milk, 15 *VICESIMUS KNOX* to bewail every new birth as an increase of misery under a government where the mind is necessarily debased and talents are seduced to become the panegyrists† of usurpation and tyranny.

16 *SAMUEL LANGDON* We have lived to see the time when liberty is just ready to expire; when the constitution of government which has so long been the glory and strength of our nation is deeply undermined and ready to tumble into ruins; when America is threatened with cruel oppression and the arm of power is stretched out to compel us to submit to the arbitrary acts of legislators who will not bear the least part of the burdens which, without mercy, they are laying upon us.

17 *GEORGE WASHINGTON* The time is now near at hand which must determine whether Americans are to be freemen or slaves; whether we are to have any property we can call our own; whether our

---

† Panegyrists: someone who speaks or writes in high praise of.

houses and farms are to be pillaged and destroyed, and we ourselves consigned to a state of wretchedness from which no human efforts will deliver us.

[18] *JOSIAH QUINCY* The scene is unpleasant to the eye, but it's contemplation will be useful if our thoughts terminate with judgment, resolution, and spirit. If at this period of public affairs, we do not think, deliberate, and determine *like men*—men of minds to conceive, hearts to feel, and virtue to *act*—what are we to do? To gaze upon our bondage while our enemies throw about firebrands, arrows, and death, and play their tricks of desperation with the gambols of sport and wantonness?

[19] *HENRY ARMITT BROWN* There shall be darkness in the days to come, danger for our courage, temptation for our virtue, doubt for our faith, suffering for our fortitude, a thousand shall fall before us and tens of thousands at our right hand. The years shall pass beneath and century follow century in quick succession. The generations of men shall come and go, the greatness of yesterday shall be forgotten today, and the glories of this noon shall vanish before tomorrow's sun; but America shall not perish but endure while the spirit of her fathers animates their sons.

[20] *GEORGE MASON* Let us charge our sons never to let the motives of private interest or ambition influence them to betray, nor the fear of danger or of death deter them from asserting the liberty of their country and endeavoring to transmit to their posterity those sacred rights to which they themselves were born. [21] *ROBERT INGERSOLL* Let their hearts be filled with gratitude, with thankfulness to all the heroes, to all the thinkers, to all the wise, the good, the brave of every land, whose thoughts and deeds have given freedom to the sons of men. And then let us pray that our sons would grasp the torch that these men had held and hold it high, that light

might conquer darkness still.

22 *ANDREW JACKSON* Who are we? And for what are we going to fight? Are we the titled slaves of George III? The military conscripts of Napoleon the Great? Or the frozen peasants of the Russian Czar? No! We are the free born sons of America, the citizens of the only republic now existing in the world, and the only people on earth who possess rights, liberties, and property which they dare call their own!

23 *FREDERICK DOUGLASS* My friends, power concedes nothing without a demand. It never did, and it never will. Find out just what people will submit to, and you have found out the exact amount of injustice and wrong which will be imposed upon them; and these will continue until they have resisted with either words or blows, or with both.

24 *SAMUEL ADAMS* I hope and believe that I live in a country, the people of which are too intelligent and too brave to submit to tyrants; that they never will betray the least want of spirit when called upon to guard their freedom. For none but they who set a just value upon the blessings of liberty are worthy to enjoy her. Your illustrious fathers were her zealous votaries;† when the blasting frowns of tyranny drove her from public view, they clasped her in their arms, cherished her in their generous bosoms, brought her safe over the rough ocean, and fixed her seat in this then dreary wilderness. They nursed her infant age with the most tender care. For her sake, they patiently bore the severest hardships; for her support, they underwent the most rugged toils; in her defense, they boldly encountered the most alarming dangers that could not damp their ardor! Whilst with one hand they broke the

---

† Votaries: devoted admirers.

stubborn glebe,[†] with the other they grasped their weapons, ever ready to protect her from danger. No sacrifice, not even their own blood, was esteemed too rich a libation for her altar. God prospered their valor; they preserved her brilliancy unsullied; they enjoyed her whilst they lived, and dying, bequeathed the dear inheritance to your care. And as they left you this glorious legacy, they have undoubtedly transmitted to you some portion of their noble spirit to inspire you with virtue to merit her and courage to preserve her. You surely cannot, with such examples before your eyes, as every page of the history of this country affords, suffer your liberties to be ravished from you by lawless force, or cajoled away by flattery and fraud.

[25] *JOSEPH WARREN* Patriots! Act worthy of yourselves! The faltering tongue of a hoary[‡] age calls on you to support your country! The lisping infant raises its suppliant hands, imploring defense against the monster! Your fathers look from their celestial seats with smiling approbation on their sons who boldly stand forth in the cause of virtue, but sternly frown upon the inhuman miscreant who, to secure the loaves and fishes to himself, would breed a serpent to destroy his children!

[26] *GEORGE WASHINGTON* My fellow countrymen, the fate of unborn millions will now depend, under God, on your courage and conduct. [27] *JOSEPH WARREN* You are to decide the important question, on which rests the happiness and liberty of millions yet unborn. [28] *SAMUEL ADAMS* Stain not the glory of your worthy ancestors, but like them, resolve never to part with your birthright, to be wise in your deliberations and determined in your exertions for the preservation of your liberties. Follow not the dictates of passion, but

---

[†] Glebe: land, fields.
[‡] Hoary: ancient.

enlist yourselves under the sacred banner of reason. [29 SAMUEL ADAMS] For when vain and aspiring men shall possess the highest seats in government, our country will stand in need of its experienced patriots to prevent its ruin!

[30 JOHN JAY] Let us banish unmanly fear and acquit ourselves like men! [31 JOHN HANCOCK] Let us nobly defend those rights which Heaven gave, and no man ought to take from us! [32 JONATHAN MAYHEW] Let every lover of God and the Christian religion—let every friend to truth and mankind—oppose this hateful monster! [33 SAMUEL ADAMS] My fellow patriots, let us disappoint the men who are raising themselves upon the ruin of this country!!!

[34 SAMUEL ADAMS] If you, with united zeal and fortitude, oppose the torrent of oppression; if you feel the true fire of patriotism burning in your breasts; if you, from your souls, despise the most gaudy dress that slavery can wear; and if you really prefer the lonely cottage, whilst blessed with liberty, to gilded palaces surrounded with the ensigns of slavery; then you may have the fullest assurance that tyranny with her accursed train will hide her hideous heads in confusion, shame, and despair. If you perform your part, you must have the strongest confidence that the same almighty Being who protected your pious and venerable forefathers, who enabled them to turn a barren wilderness into a fruitful field; [35 WILLIAM BRADFORD] who delivered them from all the perils and miseries thereof; [36 SAMUEL ADAMS] and who made bare his arms for their salvation, will still be mindful of you, their offspring.

A Parting Message From The Father Of Our Nation

GEORGE WASHINGTON Interwoven as is the love of liberty with every ligament of your hearts, no recommendation of mine is necessary to fortify or confirm the attachment.

The unity of government which constitutes you as one people is also now dear to you. It is justly so, for it is a main pillar in the edifice of your real independence, the support of your tranquility at home and your peace abroad; of your safety; of your prosperity; of that very liberty which you so highly prize. But as it is easy to foresee that, from different causes and from different quarters, much pains will be taken, many artifices employed to weaken in your minds the conviction of this truth. As this is the point in your political fortress against which the batteries of internal and external enemies will be most constantly and actively—though often covertly and insidiously—directed, it is of infinite moment that you should properly estimate the immense value of your national union to your collective and individual happiness; that you should cherish a cordial, habitual, and immovable attachment to it: accustoming yourselves to think and speak of it as of the palladium† of your political safety and prosperity; watching for its preservation with jealous anxiety; discountenancing whatever may suggest even a suspicion that it can in any event be abandoned; and indignantly frowning upon the first dawning of every attempt to alienate any portion of our country from the rest, or to enfeeble the sacred ties

---

† Palladium: something that gives protection and security.

which now link together the various parts.

Citizens of a common country, that country has a right to concentrate your affections. The name of American, which belongs to you in your national capacity, must always exalt the just pride of patriotism more than any appellation derived from local discriminations. With slight shades of difference, you have the same religion, manners, habits, and political principles. You have in a common cause fought and triumphed together; the independence and liberty you possess are the work of joint counsels and joint efforts of common dangers, sufferings, and successes.

Here every portion of our country finds the most commanding motives for carefully guarding and preserving the union of the whole. In this sense it is that your union ought to be considered as a main prop of your liberty, and that the love of the one ought to endear to you the preservation of the other.

These considerations speak a persuasive language to every reflecting and virtuous mind and exhibit the continuance of the Union as a primary object of patriotic desire. Is there a doubt whether a common government can embrace so large a sphere? Let experience solve it.

One of the expedients of party to acquire influence within particular districts is to misrepresent the opinions and aims of other districts. You cannot shield yourselves too much against the jealousies and heartburnings which spring from these misrepresentations; they tend to render alien to each other those who ought to be bound together by fraternal affection.

All obstructions to the execution of the laws, all combinations and associations under whatever plausible character, with the real design to direct, control, counteract, or awe the regular deliberation and action of the constituted authorities, are destructive of this fundamental principle and of fatal tendency.

They serve to organize faction; to give it an artificial and extraordinary force; to put, in the place of the delegated will of the nation, the will of a party, often a small but artful and enterprising minority of the community; and, according to the alternate triumphs of different parties, to make the public administration the mirror of the ill-concerted and incongruous projects of faction, rather than the organ of consistent and wholesome plans digested by common counsels and modified by mutual interests.

However parties or associations may now and then answer popular ends, they are likely, in the course of time and things, to become potent engines by which cunning, ambitious, and unprincipled men will be enabled to subvert the power of the people and to usurp for themselves the reins of government, destroying afterwards the very engines which have lifted them to unjust dominion.

Towards the preservation of your government and the permanency of your present happy state, it is requisite, not only that you steadily discountenance irregular oppositions to its acknowledged authority, but also that you resist with care the spirit of innovation upon its principles, however specious the pretexts.

Liberty itself will find in such a government, with powers properly distributed and adjusted, its surest guardian. It is indeed little else than a name, when the government is too feeble to withstand the enterprises of faction; to confine each member of the society within the limits prescribed by the laws; and to maintain all in the secure and tranquil enjoyment of the rights of person and property.

This spirit, unfortunately, is inseparable from our nature, having its root in the strongest passions of the human mind. It exists under different shapes in all governments, more or less stifled, controlled, or repressed; but, in those of the popular form, it is seen in its greatest rankness, and is truly their worst enemy.

The alternate domination of one faction over another—sharpened by the spirit of revenge natural to party dissension, which in different ages and countries has perpetrated the most horrid enormities—is itself a frightful despotism. But this leads at length to a more formal and permanent despotism. The disorders and miseries which result gradually incline the minds of men to seek security and repose in the absolute power of an individual; and sooner or later the chief of some prevailing faction, more able or more fortunate than his competitors, turns this disposition to the purposes of his own elevation on the ruins of public liberty.

It is important, likewise, that the habits of thinking in a free country should inspire caution in those entrusted with its administration, to confine themselves within their respective constitutional spheres, avoiding in the exercise of the powers of one department to encroach upon another. The spirit of encroachment tends to consolidate the powers of all the departments in one, and thus to create, whatever the form of government, a real despotism.

A just estimate of that love of power and proneness to abuse it, which predominates in the human heart, is sufficient to satisfy us of the truth of this position. The necessity of reciprocal checks in the exercise of political power—by dividing and distributing it into different depositaries and constituting each the guardian of the public weal† against invasions by the others—has been evinced by experiments ancient and modern, some of them in

---

† Weal: well-being.

our country and under our own eyes. To preserve them must be as necessary as to institute them.

If, in the opinion of the people, the distribution or modification of the constitutional powers be in any particular wrong, let it be corrected by an amendment in the way which the Constitution designates. But let there be no change by usurpation; for though this, in one instance, may be the instrument of good, it is the customary weapon by which free governments are destroyed. The precedent must always greatly overbalance in permanent evil any partial or transient benefit, which the use can at any time yield.

Of all the dispositions and habits which lead to political prosperity, religion and morality are indispensable supports. In vain would that man claim the tribute of patriotism who should labor to subvert these great pillars of human happiness, these firmest props of the duties of men and citizens. The mere politician, equally with the pious man, ought to respect and to cherish them. A volume could not trace all their connections with private and public felicity. Let it simply be asked: Where is the security for property, for reputation, for life, if the sense of religious obligation desert the oaths which are the instruments of investigation in courts of justice? And let us with caution indulge the supposition that morality can be maintained without religion. Whatever may be conceded to the influence of refined education on minds of peculiar structure, reason and experience both forbid us to expect that national morality can prevail in exclusion of religious principle.

It is substantially true that virtue or morality is a necessary spring of popular government. The rule, indeed, extends with more or less force to every species of free government. Who that is a sincere friend to it can look with indifference upon attempts to shake the foundation of the fabric?

Promote then, as an object of primary importance, institutions for the general diffusion of knowledge. In proportion as the structure of a government gives force to public opinion, it is essential that public opinion should be enlightened.

As a very important source of strength and security, cherish public credit. One method of preserving it is to use it as sparingly as possible, avoiding occasions of expense by cultivating peace, but remembering also that timely disbursements to prepare for danger frequently prevent much greater disbursements to repel it, avoiding likewise the accumulation of debt, not only by shunning occasions of expense, but by vigorous exertion in time of peace to discharge the debts which unavoidable wars may have occasioned, not ungenerously throwing upon posterity the burden which we ourselves ought to bear.

Observe good faith and justice towards all nations; cultivate peace and harmony with all. Religion and morality enjoin this conduct; and can it be, that good policy does not equally enjoin it. It will be worthy of a free, enlightened, and at no distant period, a great nation, to give to mankind the magnanimous and novel example of a people always guided by an exalted justice and benevolence. Who can doubt that, in the course of time and things, the fruits of such a plan would richly repay any temporary advantages which might be lost by a steady adherence to it? Can it be that Providence has not connected the permanent felicity of a nation with its virtue?

Against the insidious wiles of foreign influence—I conjure you to believe me, fellow citizens—the jealousy of a free people ought to be constantly awake, since history and experience prove that foreign influence is one of the most baneful foes of republican government.

In offering to you, my countrymen, these counsels of an old and affectionate friend, I dare not hope that they will make the strong and lasting impression I could wish; that they will control the usual current of the passions, or prevent our nation from running the course which has hitherto marked the destiny of nations. But if, I may even flatter myself, they may be productive of some partial benefit, some occasional good; that they may now and then recur to moderate the fury of party spirit, to warn against the mischiefs of foreign intrigue, and to guard against the impostures of pretended patriotism; then this hope will be a full recompense for the solicitude for your welfare by which they have been dictated.

Relying on its kindness in this as in other things, and actuated by that fervent love towards it, which is so natural to a man who views in it the native soil of himself and his progenitors for several generations, I anticipate with pleasing expectation that retreat in which I promise myself to realize, without alloy, the sweet enjoyment of partaking, in the midst of my fellow citizens, the benign influence of good laws under a free government, the ever-favorite object of my heart, and the happy reward, as I trust, of our mutual cares, labors, and dangers.

 President George Washington
 Farewell Address (Partial)
 1796

WWW.THEFOUNDERSUSA.COM

Dear Reader,

Thank you for reading *The Founders' Speech To Save America*. If you enjoyed the book, please consider sharing your thoughts through a written book review. Reviews are the most important factor in a person's decision to read a book, so thank you in advance for taking a minute to share your thoughts at the bookseller site where you purchased the book, as well as with your friends.

If you would like a signed copy of the book, or a notification on the next book in The Founders' Speech Series, please visit www.TheFoundersUSA.com and follow @TheFoundersUSA Facebook page.

My mission, and the mission of *The Founders USA*, is to remind us all of who we are as Americans, of the founding ethos and principles of this great nation, and of the faith and virtues required in a people intent on preserving their liberties. Thank you for joining us in this critical mission.

Steven Rabb

INDEX

Adams, John 1.24–25 *(p. 15)*, 1.44 *(p. 19)*, 2.5 *(p. 23)*, 2.12 *(p. 24)*, 2.19 *(p. 25)*, 2.22 *(p. 26)*, 3.18 *(p. 37)*, 3.19–20 *(p. 38)*, 3.22 *(p. 39)*, 3.54 *(p. 44)*, 3.62 *(p. 45)*, 3.64 *(p. 45)*, 4.48–49 *(p. 52)*, 5.11 *(p. 60)*, 5.29–30 *(p. 62)*, 5.40 *(p. 65)*, 6.8 *(p. 71)*, 6.25 *(p. 78)*, 6.26 *(p. 79)*, 7.20 *(p. 90)*, 7.36 *(p. 96)*, 8.21 *(p. 103)*, 8.24 *(p. 103)*, 8.25–26 *(p. 104)*, 8.28 *(p. 105)*, 8.36 *(p. 106)*, 8.43 *(p. 109)*, 8.53 *(p. 110)*, 9.2–3 *(p. 113)*, 9.31 *(p. 117)*, 9.37 *(p. 118)*, 9.46 *(p. 120)*, 9.48 *(p. 120)*, 9.51 *(p. 120)*, 9.56 *(p. 121)*, 9.66 *(p. 129)*, 9.69 *(p. 130)*

Adams, John Quincy 8.52 *(p. 110)*

Adams, Samuel 3.13 *(p. 36)*, 3.41 *(p. 41)*, 3.44 *(p. 42)*, 4.21 *(p. 48)*, 4.27 *(p. 49)*, 5.1–2 *(p. 58)*, 5.24 *(p. 61)*, 5.46 *(p. 67)*, 5.57 *(p. 69)*, 6.10 *(p. 73)*, 6.13 *(p. 74)*, 6.19 *(p. 76)*, 6.20–21 *(p. 77)*, 6.24 *(p. 78)*, 6.28 *(p. 79)*, 7.1–4 *(p. 82)*, 7.24 *(p. 92)*, 7.46 *(p. 98)*, 8.49 *(p. 109)*, 8.50 *(p. 109)*, 9.9 *(p. 114)*, 10.24 *(p. 136)*, 10.28 *(p. 137)*, 10.29 *(p. 138)*, 10.33–34 *(p. 138)*, 10.36 *(p. 138)*

Adkins, Elizabeth 7.29 *(p. 93)*

Ames, Fisher 9.30 *(p. 117)*, 9.49 *(p. 120)*

Andrews, John 6.22–23 *(p. 77)*

Anonymous 7.28 *(p. 92)*, 9.65 *(p. 129)*

Aquinas, Thomas 2.9 *(p. 24)*, 2.11 *(p. 24)*, 4.13 *(p. 47)*

Augustine of Hippo 2.10 *(p. 24)*, 4.45 *(p. 52)*

Bancroft, George 10.5 *(p. 131)*

Bastiat, Frédéric 4.43 *(p. 51)*, 5.27 *(p. 61)*, 5.42 *(p. 66)*, 5.45 *(p. 67)*, 5.48–49 *(p. 68)*, 6.4 *(p. 70)*, 9.21 *(p. 115)*, 9.23 *(p. 115)*

Beccaria, Cesare 5.13 *(p. 60)*

Beecher, Henry Ward 3.3 *(p. 34)*, 5.60 *(p. 69)*

Belloc, Hilaire 5.7 *(p. 59)*

Bible 4.12 *(p. 47)*, 5.31 *(p. 62)*, 5.32 *(p. 63)*, 5.50 *(p. 68)*, 5.53–55 *(p. 68)*

Black, Hugo 4.16 *(p. 47)*

Blackstone, William 4.5 *(p. 46)*, 4.20 *(p. 48)*

Boston Proposal 7.13 *(p. 87)*

Boyle, John 6.11 *(p. 73)*

Bradford, William 1.1–2 *(p. 9)*, 10.35 *(p. 138)*

Brooks, Phillips 3.43 *(p. 42)*

Brown, Henry Armitt 10.7 *(p. 132)*, 10.19 *(p. 135)*

Burke, Edmund 2.6 *(p. 24)*, 3.17 *(p. 37)*, 4.32 *(p. 49)*, 5.6 *(p. 59)*, 9.12 *(p. 114)*, 9.17 *(p. 114)*, 9.19 *(p. 115)*

Carpenter, M.H. 3.24 *(p. 39)*

Chambers, John 1.26 *(p. 16)*

Chambers, Oswald 4.8 *(p. 47)*

Channing, W.E. 7.44 *(p. 97)*

Chesterton, G.K. 9.61 *(p. 128)*

Cicero 5.15 *(p. 60)*, 5.17 *(p. 60)*, 9.25 *(p. 116)*

Clark, Abraham 8.31 *(p. 105)*

Cole, Nathan 1.17 *(p. 12)*

Committees of Correspondence and Towns (various) 7.5 *(p. 83)*, 7.7–8 *(p. 84)*, 7.9–10 *(p. 85)*, 7.11 *(p. 86)*, 7.16 *(p. 89)*, 7.17–19 *(p. 90)*, 8.3–5 *(p. 100)*, 8.6–13 *(p. 101)*, 8.14–17 *(p. 101)*

Constitution 4.65 *(p. 54)*, 5.18 *(p. 60)*

Cooke, Samuel 9.6 *(p. 113)*, 9.10 *(p. 114)*

Coolidge, Calvin 1.34 *(p. 18)*

Cooper, Samuel 9.1 *(p. 112)*, 9.7 *(p. 113)*

Coxe, Tench 4.46 *(p. 52)*

de Crèvecoeur, Michel Guillaume Jean 4.18 *(p. 47)*

Crockett, Davy 9.59 *(p. 121)*

Curran, John Philpot 4.70 *(p. 55)*

Declaration of Independence 8.44 *(p. 109)*

Dickinson, John 4.1 *(p. 46)*, 4.3 *(p. 46)*, 5.4 *(p. 59)*, 6.9 *(p. 72)*, 6.12 *(p. 74)*, 9.62 *(p. 128)*, 10.8 *(p. 132)*

Disraeli, Benjamin 3.38 *(p. 41)*

Douglas, William O. 9.15 *(p. 114)*, 9.8 *(p. 114)*

Douglass, Frederick 5.47 *(p. 67)*, 10.23 *(p. 136)*

Dwight, Timothy 1.49 *(p. 20)*, 5.37–38 *(p. 64)*, 5.39 *(p. 65)*

Edwards, Jonathan 1.10 *(p. 10)*, 1.12–13 *(p. 11)*, 1.20–23 *(p. 15)*, 1.46–47 *(p. 20)*, 5.43 *(p. 66)*

Eliot, George 2.16 *(p. 25)*, 2.18 *(p. 25)*

INDEX

Field, Stephen 2.7 *(p. 24)*
First Continental Congress 7.15 *(p. 88)*
Frank, William 8.38–40 *(p. 108)*
Franklin, Benjamin 1.9 *(p. 10)*, 1.11 *(p. 11)*, 1.14–15 *(p. 11)*, 3.46–47 *(p. 42)*, 3.48–53 *(p. 43)*, 3.55 *(p. 44)*, 3.58–59 *(p. 44)*, 3.61 *(p. 45)*, 7.37 *(p. 96)*, 8.46 *(p. 109)*
Fulton, Sarah 7.25 *(p. 92)*
Gerry, Eldridge 8.22 *(p. 103)*
Goodrich, Samuel 2.27 *(p. 29)*
Gray, Harrison 6.15 *(p. 76)*
Greene, Nathanael 3.7 *(p. 35)*
Hamilton, Alexander 2.20 *(p. 26)*, 3.57 *(p. 44)*, 4.52 *(p. 52)*, 5.14 *(p. 60)*, 5.16 *(p. 60)*, 6.27 *(p. 79)*, 7.6 *(p. 83)*, 9.67 *(p. 129)*, 9.68 *(p. 130)*
Hancock, John 1.40 *(p. 19)*, 7.32 *(p. 95)*, 7.41 *(p. 97)*, 8.29 *(p. 105)*, 8.37 *(p. 107)*, 8.47 *(p. 109)*, 10.31 *(p. 138)*
Henry, Patrick 3.12 *(p. 36)*, 9.18 *(p. 114)*
Herbert, Auberon 5.44 *(p. 66)*
Hitchcock, Gad 4.39 *(p. 50)*, 4.40–41 *(p. 51)*, 4.75–77 *(p. 56)*
Hodgskin, Thomas 3.37 *(p. 41)*
Holland, J.G. 2.4 *(p. 23)*, 10.1 *(p. 131)*
Hooker, Richard 4.10 *(p. 47)*
Hooper, William 8.30 *(p. 105)*
Hopkins, Stephen 8.32 *(p. 105)*
Howard, Simeon 10.9–10 *(p. 133)*
Ingersoll, Charles 2.23 *(p. 27)*
Ingersoll, Robert 10.21 *(p. 135)*
Jackson, Andrew 10.22 *(p. 136)*
Jay, John 10.30 *(p. 138)*
Jefferson, Thomas 1.41 *(p. 19)*, 3.39 *(p. 41)*, 3.56 *(p. 44)*, 4.6 *(p. 46)*, 4.7 *(p. 47)*, 4.14 *(p. 47)*, 4.17 *(p. 47)*, 4.24 *(p. 48)*, 4.34 *(p. 50)*, 4.56 *(p. 53)*, 4.62 *(p. 54)*, 4.66 *(p. 54)*, 4.68 *(p. 55)*, 4.81 *(p. 57)*, 5.3 *(p. 59)*, 5.8 *(p. 59)*, 5.25 *(p. 61)*, 5.35 *(p. 63)*, 6.3 *(p. 70)*, 6.5 *(p. 70)*, 8.35 *(p. 106)*, 9.11 *(p. 114)*, 9.28 *(p. 116)*, 9.36 *(p. 118)*, 9.40–44 *(p. 119)*, 9.45 *(p. 120)*, 9.47 *(p. 120)*, 9.50 *(p. 120)*, 9.63 *(p. 128)*, 10.3 *(p. 131)*, 10.6 *(p. 132)*

Kant, Immanuel 4.11 *(p. 47)*

Kingsley, Charles 10.2 *(p. 131)*

Knox, Vicesimus 10.15 *(p. 134)*

Langdon, Samuel 10.16 *(p. 134)*

Lee, Richard Henry 4.22 *(p. 48)*, 8.18–19 *(p. 102)*, 8.20 *(p. 102)*

Lincoln, Abraham 1.30 *(p. 18)*, 2.2 *(p. 23)*, 2.25 *(p. 29)*

Locke, John 3.5 *(p. 34)*, 4.9 *(p. 47)*, 4.19 *(p. 48)*, 4.23 *(p. 48)*, 4.44 *(p. 52)*, 5.9 *(p. 59)*, 6.2 *(p. 70)*

Madison, James 1.43 *(p. 19)*, 4.25 *(p. 49)*, 4.26 *(p. 49)*, 4.28–29 *(p. 49)*, 4.31 *(p. 49)*, 4.35 *(p. 50)*, 4.47 *(p. 52)*, 4.72–73 *(p. 55)*, 4.78 *(p. 57)*, 9.54 *(p. 120)*, 9.60 *(p. 128)*

Marshall, John 9.52 *(p. 120)*

Mason, George 3.36 *(p. 41)*, 10.20 *(p. 135)*

Maxson, Charles 1.5 *(p. 10)*, 1.7–8 *(p. 10)*

Mayhew, Jonathan 5.5 *(p. 59)*, 6.6 *(p. 70)*, 10.32 *(p. 138)*

McKean, Thomas 8.41 *(p. 108)*

Milton, John 9.27 *(p. 116)*

Minutemen Covenant 7.31 *(p. 95)*

Mises, Ludwig von 9.22 *(p. 115)*

Montesquieu 6.1 *(p. 70)*

Monroe, James 3.45 *(p. 42)*, 8.51 *(p. 110)*

Moody, D.L. 5.52 *(p. 68)*

Morris, Gouverneur 1.28 *(p. 17)*, 3.8 *(p. 35)*, 3.16 *(p. 37)*, 5.33 *(p. 63)*, 5.56 *(p. 69)*

Morris, Robert 2.8 *(p. 24)*, 2.14 *(p. 25)*, 2.17 *(p. 25)*

Newspaper 6.30 *(p. 80)*, 7.26–27 *(p. 92)*

Niles, Nathaniel 7.47 *(p. 98)*

Owen, John 5.51 *(p. 68)*

Paine, Thomas 2.1 *(p. 23)*, 4.38 *(p. 50)*, 4.50–51 *(p. 52)*, 5.10 *(p. 60)*, 5.34 *(p. 63)*, 7.48 *(p. 98)*, 9.38 *(p. 118)*, 9.58 *(p. 121)*

Pendleton, Edmund 4.63 *(p. 54)*

Polybius 9.32 *(p. 117)*

Quincy, Josiah 1.4 *(p. 9)*, 4.37 *(p. 50)*, 5.12 *(p. 60)*, 6.14 *(p. 75)*, 6.16–18 *(p. 76)*, 7.14 *(p. 88)*, 7.33 *(p. 96)*, 7.35 *(p. 96)*, 7.38–40 *(p. 96)*, 10.13 *(p. 133)*, 10.18 *(p. 135)*

INDEX

Ramsay, David 7.21 *(p. 90)*

Reed, Alexander 3.42 *(p. 41)*

Reed, Esther 7.23 *(p. 91)*

Resolution for Independence 8.23 *(p. 103)*

Robertson, F.W. 9.4 *(p. 113)*

Robeson, George M. 5.59 *(p. 69)*

Rodney, Caesar 8.42 *(p. 108)*

Roosevelt, Teddy 9.26 *(p. 116)*

Rush, Benjamin 1.31–32 *(p. 18)*, 1.42 *(p. 19)*, 3.10 *(p. 35)*, 3.34 *(p. 41)*, 8.45 *(p. 109)*, 8.48 *(p. 109)*

Savonarola, Girolamo 5.58 *(p. 69)*

Sherman, Roger 1.38–39 *(p. 18)*

Seneca 10.4 *(p. 131)*

Sigourney, Lydia 2.3 *(p. 23)*, 2.29 *(p. 29)*

Smith, Temperance 7.30 *(p. 93)*

Sons of Liberty 6.29 *(p. 80)*, 6.31 *(p. 81)*

Spencer, Herbert 4.33 *(p. 50)*

Spooner, Lysander 4.36 *(p. 50)*

Story, Joseph 1.27 *(p. 16)*, 1.33 *(p. 18)*, 1.35 *(p. 18)*, 2.26 *(p. 29)*, 2.28 *(p. 29)*, 3.63 *(p. 45)*, 4.54–55 *(p. 53)*, 4.67 *(p. 55)*

Svinin, Paul 1.16 *(p. 11)*

Swing, David 3.14 *(p. 36)*, 3.23 *(p. 39)*

Thornton, Matthew 8.33 *(p. 106)*

de Tocqueville, Alexis 2.24 *(p. 27)*, 4.2 *(p. 46)*, 4.4 *(p. 46)*, 4.30 *(p. 49)*, 4.71 *(p. 55)*, 4.74 *(p. 56)*, 5.26 *(p. 61)*, 5.28 *(p. 61)*, 5.41 *(p. 66)*, 9.20 *(p. 115)*, 9.24 *(p. 115)*, 9.29 *(p. 116)*, 9.33 *(p. 118)*

Tracy, Joseph 1.6 *(p. 10)*

Tucker, George 4.42 *(p. 51)*

Tytler, Alexander Fraser 9.34–35 *(p. 118)*

Upshur, Abel 9.53 *(p. 120)*, 9.55 *(p. 120)*

U.S. Code 18-2381 5.19 *(p. 61)*

Virginia Legislature 7.12 *(p. 87)*

Warren, Joseph 6.7 *(p. 71)*, 8.1 *(p. 99)*, 10.25 *(p. 137)*, 10.27 *(p. 137)*

Warren, Mercy Otis 4.15 *(p. 47)*, 10.11–12 *(p. 133)*, 10.14 *(p. 134)*

Washington, George 1.36–37 *(p. 18)*, 2.21 *(p. 26)*, 2.30–32 *(p. 32)*, 3.2 *(p. 34)*, 3.60 *(p. 45)*, 4.59 *(p. 53)*, 4.60–61 *(p. 54)*, 4.64 *(p. 54)*, 5.20–23 *(p. 61)*, 5.36 *(p. 63)*, 8.2 *(p. 99)*, 9.39 *(p. 119)*, 10.17 *(p. 134)*, 10.26 *(p. 137)*

Washington, Mary 2.33 *(p. 33)*

Webster, Daniel 1.29 *(p. 17)*, 1.45 *(p. 19)*, 3.1 *(p. 34)*, 3.9 *(p. 35)*, 3.11 *(p. 35)*, 3.15 *(p. 36)*, 3.21 *(p. 39)*, 3.25 *(p. 39)*, 3.26–30 *(p. 40)*, 3.31–33 *(p. 40)*, 3.35 *(p. 41)*, 3.40 *(p. 41)*, 4.57–58 *(p. 53)*, 4.69 *(p. 55)*, 4.79–80 *(p. 57)*, 7.34 *(p. 96)*, 7.43 *(p. 97)*, 7.45 *(p. 98)*, 8.27 *(p. 105)*, 8.54 *(p. 111)*, 9.13–14 *(p. 114)*, 9.16 *(p. 114)*, 9.57 *(p. 121)*, 9.64 *(p. 129)*

Webster, Noah 3.4 *(p. 34)*, 4.53 *(p. 53)*, 9.5 *(p. 113)*

West, Samuel 7.42 *(p. 97)*

Whipple, William 8.34 *(p. 106)*

White, Emerson 3.6 *(p. 34)*

Whitefield, George 1.18–19 *(p. 14)*, 1.48 *(p. 20)*

Williams, Samuel 2.13 *(p. 25)*, 2.15 *(p. 25)*

Winthrop, Hannah 7.22 *(p. 91)*

Winthrop, John 1.3 *(p. 9)*

Made in the USA
Columbia, SC
05 July 2025